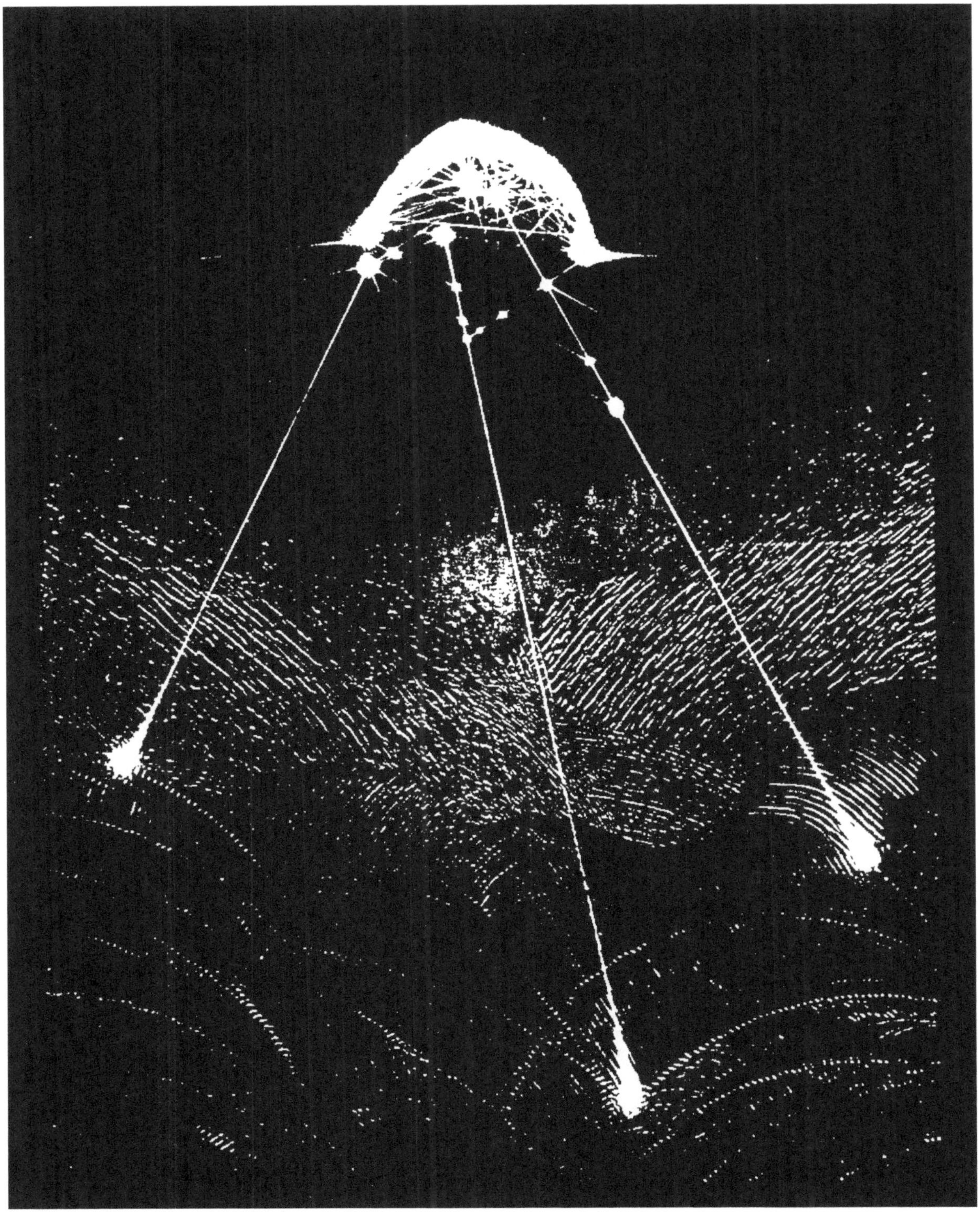

Will we recognize the beings from the more advanced planets when they appear?

UP RAINBOW HILL

by

Dana Howard

Introduction by Regan Lee

UP RAINBOW HILL

by
Dana Howard

Nonfiction

No part of this book may be reproduced, stored in retrieval system or transmitted in any form or by any means, electronic, mechanical, photocopying, recording, without express permission of the publisher.

Copyright ©2009/2014

Timothy Green Beckley: Editorial Director
Carol Rodriguez: Publishers Assistant
Sean Casteel: Associate Editor
Cover Art: Carol Ann Rodriguez
Design, layout and format: William Kern

Printed in the United States of America

For free catalog write: Conspiracy Journal
P.O. Box 753 New Brunswick, NJ 08903

Free Subscription to Conspiracy Journal
E-Mail Newsletter www.conspiracyjournal.com

UP RAINBOW HILL

DANA HOWARD

CONTENTS

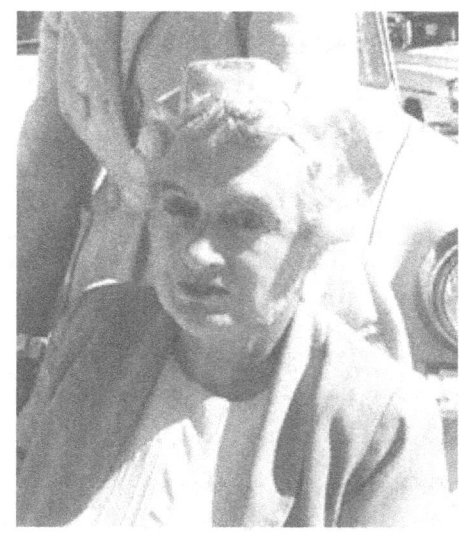

Dana Howard at a gathering of UFO enthusiasts at Giant Rock

Giant Rock in the California desert, cracked like a huge egg

Introduction

The Mystical Contactee Encounters of Dana Howard

by Regan Lee

There aren't as many female contactees of the Golden Age of UFOs as there are male, but there are a few. One was Dana Howard, who wrote about her encounters in My Flight to Venus (1956), Diane: She Came From Venus (1956), Over the Threshold (1957), Vesta, the Earthborn Venusian (1959), as well as others. As we can see, Howard was a prolific writer! (Daniel Fry, another contactee, had a short announcement in his newsletter, **Understanding**, about Dana Howard's appearances in California.) (In that same issue is a letter from contactee Orfeo Angelucci!)

While I'm intrigued by the contactees in general, and realize there are many perspectives and theories surrounding "what really happened," I'd like to focus on the symbolic of Howard's experience, rather than attempt to prove or disprove her experience. What stood out for me as I read about Dana Howard's accounts were the similarities to Marian Apparitions. Howard's experiences seemed to be a blend of space age contactee encounters, complete with flying saucers, and some of the characteristics of appearances of the Virgin Mary.

1939: The First Encounter

"Still wrapped in the warm intoxication of the spirit, my vision was directed to a gnarled old tree overlooking the antediluvian hills. Leaning casually against the grotesque trunk was a woman being of unsurpassed loveliness. Her head was radiant with a crown of fire, strands of golden hair cascading gently over her beautiful, slightly olive-tinted shoulders. The strange mystic light flooding her dark, prophetic eyes, added a wistful something to all her other charms."

Similar in ways to reports of seeing the entity, Mary. But the sighting turns space age, for Howard follows Diane into a flying saucer: ". . . a beautiful rocket-shaped ship suspended in mid-air about three hundred feet from the earth. . . In the main it seemed to be constructed of some sort of translucent materials, but trimmed in gold, and gem-studded. An almost invisible "ladder" extended from the ship to the earth, and I obediently followed the radiant being up the filmy stairs without question. Once aboard, my sacrosanct companion vanished, and I never saw her again."

Sixteen Years Later

In 1955, sixteen years after the first encounter, Diane the Venusian appeared for the second time, this time during a séance. The séance was conducted by a well known medium at the time, Reverend Bertie Lillie Candler, in Los Angeles, California. An eight foot tall female figure, described as being very beautiful, appeared before them. Howard describes the materialization:

I saw a rising glow of phosphorescence. It was very tall at first, but out of this phosphorescent substance a form began to manifest itself. She was definitely different from the other "spirit" manifestations, a solid, fleshly being, delicate in charm and manner.

I'm reminded again of some parallels to Marian apparitions. (After Diane appeared, she changed her appearance from the eight foot tall being to a more human like five foot tall being.)

The female entity said she was the same Diane from Venus that Dana had met sixteen years ago, and was responsible for giving Dana telepathic messages during that time. Like most of the other good looking humanoid beings of the Contactee era, she imparted messages of the importance of spiritual growth, transformation of both body and psyche, and eventual life on Venus.

What did Diane, the Venusian, have to say to Dana? Diane referred to

Dana as "my daughter." (alternately calling her 'child of earth') several times, for example:

"My daughter always remember: without inner perfection there can be no outer perfection. There must be perfect balance between the realm of spirit and the realm of materiality.

Materialization at the Séance

At the séance in Los Angeles, Dana Howard wasn't the only witness; there were many others who verified seeing the entity.

Dana Howard's account of the "materialization séance" follows:

Reverend Bertie Lillie Candler, proclaimed by many as the greatest physical medium of the world was holding a private séance at the church of Divine Light, 837 South Parkview Street, Los Angeles, California.

I had never attended a materialization séance before, and my inquiring mind asked all sorts of questions. As my cerebral atoms whirled with curiosity, toward the close of the meeting the "little white church" seemed.to me electrified with a powerful vibration.

Then, some ten or twelve feet from the draped-off area where Reverend Candler was in deep trance, I saw a rising glow of phosphorescence. It was very tall at first, but out of this phosphrorescent substance a form began to manifest itself. She was definitely different from the other "spirit" manifestations, a solid, fleshly being, delicate in charm and manner.

she called for Dana. Overwhelmed with emotion I could not choke back, I went up to her, standing only inches away from the manifestation. White I did not recognize her instantly, I knew there was something quaintly familiar about her. Standing like a sylphlike goddess, and bowing low in greeting to the twenty-seven persons present, the rich tones of her voice vibrated through the little church.

"I am Diane. I come from Venus."

Witnesses

Witness Lucile Points ,present at the séance, said:

A beautiful, fleshly being came, rather hesitantly at first, then saying, 'l am Diane. I come from Venus.' Since I was sitting next to the draped-off place I greeted this beautiful one asking: 'With whom do you wish to speak?' She replied softly: 'I wish to speak with Dana.'

There were other witnesses as well:

"On April 29, 1955, the writer, Mrs. Gladys Campbell and my friend, Mrs. Maude Haas, attended a materialization séance at the Church of Divine Light, 837 South Parkview Street, Los Angeles, California . . . the medium being Reverend Bertie Lillie Candler of Florida, one of the foremost materialization mediums of this country.

"I am more than happy to give an account of what I witnessed to the best of my recollection, and you will recall, when you spoke at the Pyramid Church in Alhambra the following Sunday after the visit, I was the one who got up and verified your statements concerning the visit of Diane.

"It was truly a marvelous thing to be present and see for myself such a wonderful personality, and I know you must be very humble and gratified to have the facts that you brought before the public in your book, 'My Flight to Venus', substantiated in such an unexpected manner."

—Mrs. Gladys Campbell

There were many other witnesses that day who also wrote letters confirming their experience.

Symbolism

It's interesting Diane said she came from Venus, for Venus of course is the planet representing the female sex, fertility, beauty, love. It is the morning and the evening star. Diane gave many messages on love to Dana Howard:

"Child of Earth . . . try to listen through space for the voice of one who has not forgotten. Try to make every breath, a breath of love.

Try to make every word, a word of love. Make every act an act of love. To do so, is to love and be loved. When you find the great jewel of love in your heart, you will find also as you walk down the streets of life, the good and the noble in every soul you meet.

The name Diane, a form of Diana, means the Divine. So we have a Divine Love from the heavens, appearing to an earthling with messages of love, creativity, and the need for constructive transformation; raising the self up to a higher vibration.

The symbolism in these encounters is interesting. Was it a true encounter with an alien? Or the same presence that is manifest in appearances of the Virgin Mary? It is interesting the experience took place during a séance; a perfect setting for manifestations of all kinds of spirits and entities; including some part of Dana Howard herself that was Diane. We don't know and probably never will know if Dana Howard's experiences were some kind of subliminal, paranormal experience, or if she made the whole thing up. (but what of witnesses?)

The following item is very interesting, for its church setting and the relation to Marian apparitions, and the desert setting for contactee experiences:

The appearance of the lovely Diane in the "little white church in Los Angeles" is only one side of the miracle that occurred on April 29, 1955. Out on the desert where your author resides during resort season, another miracle had happened. Mrs. Barbara MacDonald, a member of the Ground Observation Corp, a civilian agency attached to the Air Force reported that her skywatchers had broadcast four strange ships seen high in the desert skies during the week of Diane's visitation. There was no chance for error here.

There were other witnesses to the ships in the desert skies. These ships were reported as having portholes, made no sound, traveled at great speed, and disappeared before their eyes.

Other sightings by witnesses took place at Desert Hot Springs in California over several days.

Venusian, Mary, or Both?

Howard's first encounter with Diane, in 1939, took place outdoors, in the country, a usual setting for Marian apparitions. Dana's description recalls some of the descriptions from witnesses to Mary:

Her head was radiant with a crown of fire, strand.s of golden hair cascading gently over her beautiful, slightly olive-tinted shoulders. The strange mystic light flooding her dark, prophetic eyes, added a wistful something to all her other charms.

The entity appearing at Fatima was seen above a tree. young Bernadette saw what she called a "Lady in White' at Lourdes, appearing in a grotto. Several descriptions of Marian apparitions, going back centuries to the present, often include reports of the being bathed in white light.

The Contactee Era

It's always interesting to find information on a contactee from that era. This episode has many similar qualities to other Contactee experiences, along with some contrasts. The Venusian, good looking in appearance, imparting messages of love and health and healing are common. There were witnesses to the event; as happens in both some of the contactee encounters, and Marian Apparitions. But the way the being appeared to Dana Howard, and the symbolic nature of this encounter make this a bit different. The two females, the feminine and divine in the symbology, white light, and church setting seem to parallel Marian apparitions more than contactee encounters. Yet, the entity did not say she was from "Heaven" but Venus, and there were other witnesses to sightings of flying saucers in the California desert.

Was what Dana Howard the same force behind Marian apparitions and many UFO/contactee events? Possibly. Some researchers have suggested this over the years.

Whatever "really" happened, the Dana Howard encounter is certainly a highly interesting case!

Who Is Regan Lee?

Regan Lee is a UFO witnesses and writes on her own UFO related sightings and experiences, as well as the uFo phenomena in general.

Regan's interests are not limited to the UFO phenomena, but include paranormal, cryptozoological and esoteric subjects.

Among her interests are Mothman, Bigfoot, mind control, MIBS, UFO lore, the contactee movement, the abduction phenomena, Trickster element within UFOlogy, female contactees, the UFOs in context of religious and BVM encounters, mysticism, astral journeys, folk religion and beliefs, folk art, UFO and paranormal encounters in Oregon, cattle mutilations and UADs unexplained animal deaths), MILABS, reptilians, ancient astronaut theory, ghosts, mediumship, hauntings, the Trickster in UFology, UFology as culture.

Regan's blogs include: Vintage UFO, Saucer Sightings, The Orange Orb.

Diane

FOREWORD

The age of SPACE is here. It was ushered in more than a decade ago with electrifying spectacle and provocative fanfare. Strange, cylindrical objects traversed the skies from one end of the globe to the other. Their inscrutable behavior pattern was not only mystifying, it baffled the most discerning minds. It was not easy to accept the possibility that extra-terrestrials had entered our atmosphere—that perhaps the sphere-shaped objects had come millions-of miles across space from some remote point in our solar system.

As they came in greater numbers the credibility grew on the one hand, skepticism mounted on the other. Time passed and humanity became "thought-divided." A parallel was seen with the story of the beginning of the Christian Era. Skeptics were ready to throw believers into a den of lions. The believers prayed to God that the time would come when all must believe.

When we trace the line of history, we find that the harbingers of the future have had many similarities. Each major change is ushered in with the mysterious. The mysteries are always with us. If an event proves to be inspirationally interesting, it lives. If it is daring, if it is challenging, others are inspired and impassioned to carry on. They are ready to make every sacrifice, spending every precious moment delving deeper through the sub-soil until they have found an answer. With an established base and enthusiastic nucleus, life is ready to go on to a new spiral.

In the past decade many have claimed contact with beings from outer space. Some believe these visitors to be physical like ourselves. But they have been taught to measure all things on an earthly yardstick. They attempt to ignore that which is abstruse. Their vision is blinded to the insoluble. At the same time these people are faced with a paradox. The cylindrical objects are Earthly one moment, yet they vanish into nothingness the next. While these people resent the alien, they are forced to admit this fact.

The believers are sometimes effusive in their claims. Their stories are festooned with enthusiasm for they seem to burn within with some strange emotion. In their bombastic efforts to spread the message many have done more harm than good.

On the other hand, the middle-road can lead us to the correct answers.As intelligent beings we know that space cannot be measured by an Earth yardstick. I have felt from the beginning that other-worldly beings are in all aspects similar to us in appearance and that they have the ability to materialize or dematerialize at will, They are weightless beings, free from the pull of gravity.

The illustrious Carl Jung is said to have stated: "I believe the UFOS are real and show signs of intelligent guidance by guasi-human pilots."

In a recent lecture tour through Europe, George Hunt Williamson, world explorer and UFO researcher stated: "Appearances of a beautiful lady in bright light (similar to Our Lady of Fatima) have been reported from various parts of Italy." Documented cases of similar nature appear in this book and they all tie in with the description of the Radiant One known to my readers as the inimitable Diane. Since her first appearance in 1939, she has come through the veil many times. It would seem such facets of the "Feminine-Principle" have been coming through the ages. Are they in reality beings from other planets? This is something we hope to prove in the near future.

At the completion of my book, "Over the Threshold," Diane's direct mediatorship terminated. She explained that "channelship" had been established; phenomena had played their dramatic roles, and henceforth I would be permitted to "tap" direct knowledge without the aid of a mediator. "Up Rainbow Hill" (for the most part) is channeled material.

The flying saucer era has passed, and with it the spectacle. It has not gone into oblivion, but rather has been metamorphosed into a living, vital Space Age. This is the story of the BREAKTHROUGH.

Dana Howard, December, 1958

Appearance of a Mothership

Conspiracy Journal
PRODUCTIONS

I

CHAPTER ONE

"I do set MY BOW in the cloud, and it shall be for a token of a Covenant between Me and the Earth."-Gen. 9:13.

It was a day of electrifying intensity and every cell in my body throbbed to a beat of strange ecstasy. I stopped the car and pulled over close to the cactus-studded terrain of the desert. There I sat, quietly meditating on the serenity of the two majestic peaks in the distance: the peaceful, eternally feminine San Gorgonio, the masculine and rugged San Jac. They were like twin souls that had come up through a cycle of time and were now ready to reveal their innermost secrets. There had always seemed a warm tie of affection between these two giant monoliths standing noble and erect, guardians over the enchanting sandy wastes below.

My mortal gaze came to rest upon a bow of celestial glory as it cast an effulgence of magenta-hued glow over the clean, wind-washed sand. A rainbow in the desert! There was no moisture in the atmosphere, no indication of desert showers. The iridescent tints there in the solitude of nature brought lyrics to my soul. Surely this was what the poet meant when he said: "When we can live in the colors of the rainbow, we can play in the rolling clouds."

UP RAINBOW HILL

I had seen many arcs of glory out here in nature's wonderland, but never a rainbow like this. The torso of a great sand hill was literally bathed in a diffusion of colored light. But I was soon to know that I was being wrapped in some mystical portent. One day, every inch of the Planet Earth would be bathed in this glorious mist. It would be the day of the change—the breakthrough from an earth-cycle to a cycle of space. With it would come purification, regeneration. . . renewal. This would be the day of which the world had been waiting throughout history.

I knew then, as others before me had known, that the rainbow is a symbol of revelation; the gateway between the visible and invisible worlds. Through the centuries it had been written that one day the earth would make a bright new start. There would be an expansion of awareness; a dimensional increase such as we had never known before. The people of earth would be freed from their ropes of bondage. A long and suffering cycle would come to an end.

Hundreds of centuries ago, somewhere along the pathway, humanity had lost its way. Through the wearying centuries the pendulum had been swinging first to one extreme, then the other. The earth was still spilling its life blood, not in wisdom but in ignorance.

I had lived through this cycle in cosmic memory. My mind often trailed back to days of the beginning. It had been a slow and arduous climb, each step frustrated with tortures and pain. Little man had to adapt to each new environment. He built his world as he went along. His first shelters were fashioned from the rocks and the trees and "the groves were his first temples." Life was sustained by the meat of wild things and the surrounding vegetation. The surface of the Earth was man's home, and for centuries he believed it to be flat. It was a nostalgic existence for his hermitage was one of exile. He often looked toward the stars at night, but it never occurred to him they, too, might be inhabited.

It was then that Earthman learned about faith. For without that mystic something deep within him he could not have endured the hardships of the upstream fight. His soul experienced few tranquil moments, there was seldom an interlude free from terror and fear. As he reached each new rung of the Earthly ladder his struggles grew with him. Eventually he became reconciled to a life of conflict and quarrels. The virus of war invaded his blood-stream.

Conflict has been the keynote of the now ending cycle. It was the way of evolution. Suffering was the molder of things to come. Suffering assumed the role of guardian of man's dreams.

Living alone, he became aware that he needed companionship. The time came when the pulse of a social sense throbbed through his veins. The urge for power was born. The weak gave way to the strong. The overlord waved a stout whip and wielded it at the least provocation. He tortured lesser man into submission. Torture became a part of the plan and purpose of existence.

With the slime and obscenity of the centuries still clinging to us, our civilization pushed slowly ahead. Leaders, drunk with power, became dots in a circle. They began to circumvent the world's wishes with greed and aggression their purpose. Through the generations, greed has generated its own vile poisons until today these poisons are devouring every last unit of humanity. The same vitriolic gases, let loose in days long ago are with us still. Living organisms have gone through countless stages of growth, but somewhere along the evolutionary line the "God-side" of man has been side-tracked. He can no longer hear the strains of celestial music. He lost touch with the heavenly hosts and the castles of gold. When he strayed from the main line he saw himself in parts, seldom in Oneness.

He specialized one part and neglected another. Eventually he lost touch with the Source of his being; the true supply of his daily bread.

This is where the great mass of humanity stands today. Earthman has placed his faith in things, not in the Source of things. The inflated egos of the majority refuse to believe there are beings more advanced than us. They want no part of the fruits of wisdom. To ask them to consider that other planetary families live in the skies is regarded by them an insult to their intelligence.

With an awakening of faith, we can again contact the symbol of faith. But we cannot place our certitude in destruction and expect construction to be the result. The scepter of destruction is in our very midst. It is the ghost we must face on every doorstep. No longer the few but every least unit of humanity is being forced to swim in this stream of soured world consciousness.

The pattern has not changed. We have marched through life, sometimes swiftly, then falteringly and at times we have been reduced to a mere crawl. Nothing short of a resurgence of faith can restore our honor toward life and living—not faith in atom bombs and the monstrosities of war, but "faith in the substance of things hoped for—the essence of things unseen. This is the faith that can save us.

"But," says the man in the street, "Only a miracle could bring along such faith." Few of us can perform miracles, to be sure but most of us do believe that we possess limitless potentialities. The miracle lies buried in the folds of our potential.

Where are we going to start? How can we transfer our faith from atom bombs to a belief in some transcendent magnanimity?

As the door of the new cycle opens, little by little the rays of light will stream in. Those who yearn to be free will find the heavy chains and binding ropes will fall away like magic.

Many are beginning to believe that a miracle occurred in 1947 when Kenneth Arnold spotted nine shining discs racing across the northwestern skies of the United States of America. The masses were stirred by curiosity and wonderment. But none realized then, and few have accepted the fact since, that a miracle had come to the Earth. Of course a whispering campaign spread the word that strangers were in our midst. And with it a little faith sprung up in the heart—faith that has grown geometrically. But the majority of humans still bathe in a sea of inertia and will not come ashore long enough to listen and learn. They do not want to budge from the rotting base of old ideas. It has been their foundation of life as long as they can remember.

More join the curious every day. They are beginning to wonder where they came from and why they are here. There are millions throughout the world who would like to join the ranks of the believers, but they must be given a satisfying answer to their questions. While people the world over have seen and photographed hundreds of these alien objects, the mystery has not been solved. No one has captured a saucer. No one has taken one apart to see what makes it tick. And so the race goes on. Those who would attempt to measure the broader dimension on the outmoded yardstick are in the race, too. But with them it is a race only to see who gets there first. They want to point with pride and say: "I put up that flag."

Whether or not we know it, we are still prospecting for gold and the things gold will buy. We are gathering more and more possessions, but we have no security. We are afraid to place our feet on the rungs of the celestial ladder, fearing it might be a mirage. But this attitude will no longer suffice, for the lure of space will not be abated much longer. The same restless suspense is churning within us all, We do not have to be told that we have merely scratched the surface of our endeavors. We know that we stand on the threshold of something more important than speeding missiles, more all-encompassing than Russian sputniks. It goes deeper into the realm of the mysteries than anything we have ever tackled.

Those who have been nurtured in this strange era have been literally hurled into a new dimension of thinking. They are well indoctrinated with the thought that, one day soon, the miracle of space travel will be a reality and in the "twinkling of an eye" they will be traveling the airways of the universe. It could be that those who jeer Ind ridicule today will owe their release to the few staunch and loyal ones who steadfastly refuse to repeat the same monotonous psychological routine over again. The new Declaration of Independence has been etched into the hearts of these dissenters. They will not align themselves with further destruction. They will want to be rid of the evils the centuries have imposed upon them. They are through forever with the psychic octopus that is devouring us—the violence that breeds more violence.

If we are willing to face facts we need not be told that if we continue in the pattern of violence the wrathful deities will do their part. For where the anger of man leaves off, the wrath of nature begins. Many cycles have come to an abrupt end through earthquakes, tornadoes and cataclysm. There is no reason to doubt that the present cycle can end that way too.

We are all contestants in the greatest race of all time. The jacket blurb of my book "Over the Threshold" says: "Our Earth is entering a new phase. We must be prepared to go along with it."

How can we prepare? The old way has been to make still more monstrous weapons for war. But even the making of war's terrible tools takes on a dull monotony in time. This machinery has worked overtime and is slowing down. The knives of industry are beginning to slash. The stockpile that has been built up since World War II is beginning to crumble. It is possible the waves of approaching destruction will reach to the tallest skyscraper.

When the fetid end comes many will be like the dog with the bone who saw his reflection in a pool. He dropped his meaty bone for the mirage that wasn't there.

This is the kind of faith that has sustained us; a misplaced faith that can be bombed out from under us with one fell swoop. At the moment of cataclysmic destruction we will discover that the threads we have so carefully woven are made of a rotted, inferior wool.

The faith our souls have cried out for is a faith we have not yet embraced. We will not find it in blind experimentation. We will not find it trying to plow through noisome decay. So long as force is sovereign we will be compelled to live by force.

The heavy layers of poisonous substance we have created through the centuries must be cleaned out, not scabbed over.

We cannot accomplish this cleansing while one camp prepares for war with a blind urge to conquer; the other plodding along the enchanted pathway, and the way of peace. Yet isn't the tranquil life something we feel in our hearts whoever and where ever we are?

Archeology and geology have helped us turn back the pages of the centuries. In the long interim man has risen from a beast to the human being he is now. He is no longer blind to his surroundings, for deep within he knows that he is one of God's children; that he came from Divine Source. In a measure he can evaluate the rich experiences he has gained. Although objectively he is still a social creature, subjectively he is a free spirit. He knows that vitality has been drained from life, that the future he faces is futile. He knows he cannot go on forever hiding his head in the sand, trying to stimulate his lagging interest with every kind of new drug.

Where can man find the true answer? He will find it in his faith: "faith in the substance of things hoped for . . . the essence of things not seen."

UP RAINBOW HILL

CHAPTER TWO

The long cycle from which we are now emerging consisted of many minor cycles. First came the period of involution—the incubation of ideas. As ideas were drawn from the founts of knowledge, they were slowly molded into realities. The faltering steps of humanity moved forward until the point of pyramiding was reached. Now where do we go from here?

Millions of humans are aware that we are playing a losing game on the cosmic chessboard. If we dare to make one more wrong move, the game is over. We will have lost the heritage for which we fought through more years than we can begin to count.

With the striking of the fatalistic gong, pioneers and questers are waking from their lethargic slumbers. They are shaking the dust from their tomb wrappings. They are daring to come out onto the stage of the theatre of life for the first time.

They are madly delving into the past; they are projecting their minds into the future. The floor of their den is strewn with yellowed newspapers and old records taken from long untouched files. They have found evidence to support "fairy tales" told by their grandmothers and grandfathers. Some of the answers have been found in the Bible and other sacred literature. For the events that seem so strange now have happened before. Many, many times before. Inspired by an unconquerable urge to delve, searchers have found mute evidence that strange spacecraft, too, have been here before. There is a veritable treasury of knowledge in these musty old volumes. The pieces fit together like a mosaic and the unquiet ghosts are on the prowl again.

The masses still refuse to believe that there may be a better way of life than the one they now have. They still insist upon feasting from the table's bitter fruits. They will tell you that if "winged messengers" are coming from others worlds, they are agents of the devil.

This is natural, for humanity has placed its faith in every rotting mold it has been offered. The masses have stumbled forward carrying the earth's graveyard on their bended backs. Jesus said: "For ye are like unto whited sepulchres which indeed appear beautiful outward, but are within full of dead man's bones."

He also said: "I go to prepare a place for you."

Would we follow Jesus to that place should He come to lead us? No! Most of us would be just as frightened of Him as we are supposed to be frightened of winged messengers. We would call Him an imposter, perhaps stone him as he was stoned before. We would feel certain He had come to rob us of our possessions, the weight of which has dragged us deep into our self-created mire.

This is the situation we face: half the world trying to capture "more grandiose possessions" and the other half dreaming of miracles they hope will happen. On the one side, paradise; on the other, a stewing brew that has lost its leaven.

But at least many of us know that we are in the throes of change; the change that came with the strange objects in our skies. Whether we know it or not, the unidentified flying objects (UFOs) have made us more science conscious. They have alerted us to the realization that more scientists are needed.

But who among us is equipped to train new scientists? At best it will be "the blind leading the blind,. Russia has worked with fevered heat toward this goal. Under her rule of strict regimentation she has made extraordinary gains. The youth of Russia has been through years of austere training. They have geared themselves to an objective and the resulting sputniks have been the first real challenge to the United States.

Sputnik sent us Americans frantically digging into our past. We searched the lives of our forebears, who worked tirelessly to build a new nation. They pulled tree stumps together. They built roads together. They moved as one, first eastward, then westward . . . then to the north and to the south. America's greatness was achieved in a relatively short time.

Our nation was founded on faith; not faith in the weapons of destruction, but faith "in the essence of things unseen." We lined up to immense ideas under the banner of freedom. And until conflict entered our charmed circle we actually cooperated with each other. We laid the groundwork for the richest legacies ever enjoyed by any people in our epoch. Men bored into the earth to find the riches nature had stored there. Nature gave in abundance. Others readied rich and unlimited agricultural and industrial resources. Out of it came the most fertile republic in the flickering light of civilization. But we fell short of what might have been.

In stepping back a few centuries we are able to gain a clearer perspective. The landing of the Pilgrims and the founding of the colonies was a vital point in our country's history. Those rugged individuals who came to our shores covered their bleeding hearts and the scars on their souls in hard work. They had dared to escape religious intolerance and to look for something which would satisfy the hunger in their hearts. They soon learned they were not to escape hardships in this new land. Severe in their own social life, they were unaware they had dragged along with them man's unhappy heritage. While they wore the cloak of virtue, they had not cleansed their auras. When the Pilgrim Fathers unlocked their iron trunks, they fished out the tradition-ridden scrolls hidden there. Almost before America was out of her swaddling clothes, she was fighting a war. It was then we began to realize that if our gains were to be held, our foundation must be made more secure. Deep within we knew that that which was gained by force would one day be taken by force.

In October 1775, George Washington, depressed in spirit and deeply apprehensive of the future, wrote to James Warren in Massachusetts:

"The war, as you have observed, has terminated most advantageously for America, and a fair field is presented to our view; but I confess to you freely, my dear sir, that I do not think we possess the wisdom or justice enough to cultivate it properly. Illiberality, jealousy and local policy mix too much in all our political councils for the good of the Union."

Again the following year, the first President of the United States expressed similar views:

"I think of our situation and view it with concern," he said. "From the high ground on which we stood, from the path which invited our footsteps, to be so fallen, so lost, is mortifying. Everything of virtue has in a degree taken its departure from our land. What a gracious God is man that there should be such inconsistencies and perfidiousness in his conduct. It was but the other day we were shedding our blood to obtain the Constitution under which we now live, and now we are unsheathing swords to overthrow it"'

America is the land where the least can become the greatest. For many years it was the rule rather than the exception that the office boy might become the president. We struggled up the hard way. We believed we were working with aim and purpose.

We wanted to be free from tyranny. Europe had wallowed in war and destruction until this had become her daily diet. The God of Hate was Europe's deus ex machina of growth.

We dare not found our Space Age on the same decadent base. It is time we destroyed the old pattern. The Washington and the Lincoln qualities of nobility have virtually vanished. The basic principles upon which we founded our nation are no longer operative. But America at least has a smaller cosmic debt to pay than her blood-soaked neighbors. The cleanest of the family of nations, it is not difficult to understand why the seeds of the New Dispensation should be sown right here in America.

In 1939 I went through a strange mystical experience which can only now be properly evaluated in the light of the many strange happenings in the world. Was it prophecy of was it fantasy? It is difficult to discern where one leaves off and the other begins, for they are joined together in unbroken wedlock. Today I refer to it as my teleportive flight to Venus. I quote here the words of the High Priest in that magnificent Temple of Venus:

"We have with us a messenger from the Planet Earth," he said, in a beautiful, rich-toned voice. "She has come to us to be taught in our schools. . . to learn something of our way of life. When she returns to her home planet she will be immersed in our high ideals. These treasures she will store away in her heart to be passed along as occasion wills.

"Child of Earth, the treasures planted on one planet in one given age are eventually reaped on other planets in the ages to come. In the days ahead the Planet Earth will draw her bountiful beauties from us, for as you have already seen, beauty is the keynote of this Land of Love.

"Your day of glory will come. The land known as America will live in richness and splendor. She will be inspired in the patterns of God's highest creations. That you might not be misled, as our people here know, we too had our rise and fall. But, our hearts now linked in brotherhood, we shall never again suffer that injustice. We shall never again know selfishness or greed. Our values, rooted in love, shall never again know malice or be subjected to ignoble acts.

"Step by step each and every planet in the broad universal system must climb the golden stairs. Your own America is the hope of your planet. She shall rise to her greatness, a haven for all who seek rest. With the coming of the New Dispensation, America, the land that has housed so many races, shall rise. Her banner of freedom shall wave in all its glory."

This was long in advance of the coming of strange spacecraft. It requires no mystic card reader to tell us that America has violated the pattern that made her great. We look back on George Washington as an inspired, forward-looking person who led our country out of the wilderness. He knew the meaning of justice. He knew that special privilege could not be given the few at the expense of the many. He knew that if our structure was to endure it must include that cohesive quality known as brotherhood.

But selfishness became our springboard of action. We tried to regulate conduct by permissive social intercourse on the one hand, severe penal codes on the other. We did not discard the old pattern, we merely patched it up. It was the pattern drafted ages ago when we were foraging for our food. This follows the thorny tradition Farthman has built. In this impervious way he developed his civilization.

We are not seeking some fantastic Utopia, but we do not wish to cling any longer to a set of withering values. The time has come to reshape our lives according to the best ideal. This ideal must be one of brotherhood. It must be an ideal of social justice, cooperation and like mindedness. These are the days when all humanity must be reset in a new frame of reference. Its mounting can be lustrous gold or tarnished brass. It will be what we make it—nothing more, nothing less.

CHAPTER THREE

We have perceived with a passing glance an infinitesimal fragment of the past. But what of the present and the future? We need no magnifying glass to see the pattern repeating itself. There is a variation in the time element; the intensity of the vicious machine has been pitched to a greater focus; the veil of security has worn thinner, but the basic pattern remains intact. The outworn form stands in its tattered garment daring us to disrobe it.

Some of us are capable of viewing that outworn form as a monster balloon. At the beginning of the age it was inflated with the substances then known to our planet. They were clean, fresh gases, for they had not yet been infected with the viruses emanating from the nauseating stupidities of man.

The gas bag grew to become a mighty civilization; the gases churned and stirred as though whipped by giant egg-beater.

Good and bad went into the same vat. With each blast of the bellows came a surge of motivating force that brought mankind ever closer to capturing the material strongholds. The driving power grew, and with it the gas bag. Inflated to its capacity, it began to burst at the sides. As each hole appeared it was quickly covered with a patch. Today those patches have become so numerous there is little of the original gas bag left. Nor is there room for many more patches. The gases have been churned and blended until only a poisonous sediment remains. That sediment is the substance upon which we are feeding. It goes without saying we cannot subsist indefinitely upon these rapidly accumulating poisons.

What can we do about it? We can create a new balloon—a balloon this time with wings, for it will have to soar into space. Whether we know it or not the new cycle is well under way. It came into being the day the Wright brothers flew; the day our first airplane sailed into the skies. When we were finally convinced that empty space would hold our weight, we were also certain that one day we would conquer gravity.

That day is close at hand. The New Heaven and the New Earth are in the birth stage. "Now that which decayeth and waxeth old is ready to vanish away," says Hebrews 8:13. We know that our destined pathway between the planets must be opened up, for God said: "Behold, I create all things new."

Many believe that extraterrestrials are in our midst. A few are convinced that these visitors are guardian angels and that they have been with us a long, long time. Some have heard the voice of warning: that still small voice that does not err. We do not have to be told that our economic structure is crumbling. Every intelligent thinker knows that an economy based on warmongering cannot endure forever. We also know that the outworn form must be replaced by something fresh and enduring. We can postpone it a little longer, perhaps, for we are a procrastinating people. But if we wait too long, the stockpile of atom bombs stored from one end of the earth to the other is sure to explode in our midst. We will be cast into oblivion without a moment to say our prayers.

It is hard to believe we have gained so little from the hard blows of experience. That we must be crumbled into the dust before we decide to act. What has become of that "certainty" we once possessed? Has it, too, been wrapped in our tarnished memories? We cannot shoot the ghosts that haunt our path. Ghosts are immune to the monstrosities of violence. But a change of pattern will send them scurrying to their tombs in short order.

Civilization has gone off the deep end. We did the best we could with our limited understanding. There is no just cause for remorse or regrets. And the eleventh hour has not yet arrived! Let us take another look at those strange discs in our skies. Despite the denials from officials and severely orthodox scientists, a large percentage of the earth believes the UFOs are there. So we have gained very little knowledge about them. We haven't been able to capture a saucer, therefore we have no concrete evidence. But must we forever deny that which we cannot capture?

That which can be seen must have an unseen side. Although ridicule is heaped upon those who would entertain a subjective point of view, we owe our new found space consciousness to this very source. The psychological effect of this "space consciousness" has opened up many new avenues of research. Whether zealots or realists, the non-conformist has furnished a literal substrata upon which we can mount our sights. The extreme loyalties to which they have clung have done their part in speeding up space travel. When we can permanently set our sights, when there is no further doubt in our minds, then perhaps we can forget war mongering long enough to help launch our Space Age in earnest.

The pattern of our thinking has not changed. The "it can't be done" theory still holds until the practicality of an idea is set before us in full operation. To comprehend the coming of things within our own world peripheries is one thing; to reach out into the unknown is another. It is virtually beyond our scope of reasoning to assume that perhaps the coming of strange spacecraft might bring us to that paradise of which we have dreamed, but in which we have never believed. It would be impossible at this time to measure the scope of what greatness is if we look upon it from an earthly vista. That which we can measure on our own little yardstick, we accept; that which we cannot measure, we reject.

Did the Russian sputniks bring us to a new state of awareness? In recognizing this "just beyondness" are we ready to give due credit to science and the future, or is it only the challenge that counts?

Russia got there first! This has created a sore spot in our thinking. The prize-fighters are in the ring; who will come out the winner? We cannot be noble so long as this childish attitude exists. Earthlings have been taught to think big, and in thinking big they have accomplished big things. But that bigness has not extended beyond the bounds of Earth. The stars above were put there to decorate the heavens and make jobs for astronomers.

UP RAINBOW HILL

We have given little thought to space travel or spacial communication. We have felt superior because we have had nothing to challenge our superiority. We have fought all new things because change interferes with our lethargies. We have clung to our doubts and despairs; we have bathed in our tears and woes just as we have clung to our worthless possessions. The tiny prisons we have made for ourselves we have padded with silks and satins. In this we are no different from the turtle living in its shell. We would stay in that self-made shell from the day of birth until the day of death unless moved out by something bigger than ourselves.

This has been the aim of war. War makes us move. But what is the point? Certainly nothing in our existence has compared to the challenge of space. To climb on the bandwagon of the miraculous is far more soul-satisfying than to contribute to the delinquency of the destructive. If it were not for the spectacular and the miraculous that appear at given intervals, the lives of human beings would be sunk deeper and deeper into the mire. Without the miraculous we would keep going on the same merry-go-round, increasing the dizzy pace to shore up our false courage.

The same pace has been applied to the war machine. We have graduated from guns and bayonets to rockets and atom bombs. No longer is it the slaughter of the fittest men, but mass murder. Nothing is sacred in modern warfare. How about those who are dedicated to destruction? Where do they go from here? They will be reduced to ash along with the rest of us, but what happens after the ashes have been deposited in the earth?

Life does not end at the grave. Nor does it end with the crumbling of the tombstone. The "invisible"' must be reckoned with. The unknown must be faced. Isn't it more interesting to anticipate a bright new world on some other planet than to wander about in the netherlands of the after-life state?

Most of us are well aware that this major change is inevitable. We cannot elect to stay where we are because the very soil upon which we stand is moving, too. Just as we are streaming into another cycle our earth is moving into another sphere.

We cannot halt individual evolution. We cannot stop the march of cosmic evolution. It goes on, ad infinitum.

But we can throw away today's yardstick. We can develop new instruments that will extend beyond the boundary line of earth. Universalism is not just an ordinary word. It is a concept that can be embraced. Perhaps we cannot open the universal doors by ourselves, but we can look to the messengers and the teachers of a higher order than we. They can help us if we cannot help ourselves. When we are ready to grow, there is always something or somebody beyond to help.

Humanity is sick and growing sicker. We are being mowed down by the epidemic of greed imposed upon us by a system we have been forced to live in; a system that has contaminated every least life unit on the Planet Earth.

We're intelligent beings, really, but we all have been deluded by false appearances. Greed is a creed built up by man. It knows nothing about principle or the application of principle. Greed is woven from the fabric of fear; it has grown into a cerebral monster that lives to devour. To give allegiance to greed is to place faith in destruction. This has been so since time immemorial. Greed does not prosper its victim in the end, but rather leaves him to wallow in a cold, psychological nakedness.

Out of this nakedness has come our sense of insecurity. Nor will we be secure so long as we live in a house built from the bricks of violence. Each day is bringing us closer to the realization that we have pledged our lives to the forces of destruction. Each wave of violence takes us a step farther away from God.

It is apparent to those whose eyes have fully opened that without moral cohesion we have but one inevitable end. It will not be the fall of man this time, but it will be the fall of all man-made schemes; the fall of his false ideologies, the fall of the system, social, civil and religious. The system must crumble or it must be transmuted. We have proven almost beyond doubt that we cannot save ourselves. So why not try to believe that beings more advanced than we might be trying to. guide our footsteps back to the promised land; back to the mainline from which we strayed eons ago.

Humanity is confused. Each person is trying to convince the other that he is right. We have reached the summit of materialization, but there is a larger, more all-embracing achievement. We have not failed and we will not fail unless we permit ourselves to succumb to the atom bomb. Greed has left us with a severe case of astral leprosy. The disease cannot be healed by heaping more poisons into the wound. Man-made gods can help destroy us, but only a superman from dimensions beyond our knowledge can teach us how to transmute.

Which path do we choose to take?

CHAPTER FOUR

We have waded through many minor cycles in the past but they have come upon us with imperceptible ease. We were scarcely aware of the shifting. But this undignified "UFO era" is different. It cannot be measured by any other cyclic span in the history of our existence. Why? Because today we are face to face with the major breakthrough.

We are still children of Earth. Few of us have ever grown up. We continue to revel in a circus and don strange raiment to celebrate the "frontier days." Now that the saucer parade has passed by, many are looking back upon it as the most colorful pageant in the fast two thousand years. We would defy drenching rains and blinding snow to stand on the curb and see it all over again. Earthlings have been taught in the ways of showmanship. If it doesn't show on the surface it is hard to arouse interest.

While Kenneth Arnold was not the first man in our history to gaze with awe at the flying discs, his experience brought out the stories of countless others who had seen something up there in the skies. The big show might have ended there, and it would soon have been forgotten. But obviously our friends from On High were not to be postponed this time. There was a plan and a purpose in their coming. We had to be alerted to that purpose.

The sightings continued on through the years. They were chalked up almost daily from all parts of the globe. This has been going on for more than a decade now, and the interest is growing rather than waning. There have been seeming periods of rest, then suddenly the activity would loom up all over again. About the time we believed they had left the skies forever, they would put on another spectacular demonstration to convince us of their reality.

Reviewing the picture as it stands, following the sighting publicity reports began to come in from obscure individuals who purportedly had seen and talked with beings from other planets. Many accepted these strange irrefutable experiences as conceivably true. Others,who had not previously been interested in life on other planets, and had not found it in their school books, dismissed the reports as the work of crackpots. The orthodox dragged out their private files to prove it. No, it wasn't in the book! It didn't add up on their mathematical slide rule. They had not seen the objects themselves, yet they dared to sit on the throne of authority. The strings of letters following their names were all they needed to slander the sighters. Oddly enough, some of the scoffers admit to a belief in little green men, one-eyed cyclopses and other monstrosities reported seen emerging from the ships. They are willing to accept the tales of little children making fantastic claims. Have thgy forgotten their own Baby Susan and that little terror Willie, who were often spanked because they came home with tales brewed in the cauldrons of their tittle imaginations? In reality, does the reluctance to investigate saucer reports not have something to do with the ego? It is difficult for many to accept the possibility of more advanced beings than ourselves. Reports have been made by many hoaxers and crackpots, to be sure, but time will sift the wheat from the chaff.

Slowly the idea of change is lodging in many minds. Even though the message has not been heard verbally or read in books, there are those who are beginning to feel that something deep within. Every new thing that happens to us is a contributing factor to the change. Those who assume the authority of leadership know it too, but trapped in the mire, often prefer to ignore it.

The rich who have lived their lives without a painful struggle for bread and meat; those who have never known the lower crusts of society, are generally satisfied with their comforts.

This plush civilization has given them the best our Earth has to offer. If there is anything better it will come to them in due time. But there are millions who are not satisfied with things as they are. They are restless with this stirring change. They are searching for a better world with nothing to lose, perhaps much to gain. These people are not taking anything away from their "plush-horse" brothers. The same violent aberration that gave the rich man his start toward the hills of gold, they are turning toward another hill; a new kind of gold. There are many shapes to the leaves on a tree—there are many new and unexplored facets of divinity. The stream of new knowledge is constantly flowing. If we are going to keep abreast of things we must learn to be adept as each new power comes along. We cannot discriminate one thing against another. In the cosmic scheme universality alone exists. Universality has no respect for nations, national borders, nor the lines that divide intelligence from ignorance. In the cosmos they are all put into the same giant mixing bowl and stirred with the same universal spoon.

How and when are we going to get back upon the main line? We talk glibly about the positive and the negative, but how many have ever understood the meaning of the these two opposing concepts? If the prison doors are to be opened, if we are to be released soon from our world bondage we must be willing to make better use of the concepts that bind us. In a measure we have tried to do this by austere self-discipline. Adepts and holy men have given themselves over to martyrdom in the cause. If our sea of life is "fouled up" the most rigorous techniques of self-discipline have only succeeded in building higher walls of isolation.

As our framework is, so are we. Until we can actually tap the larger life molds we cannot minutely follow the larger patterns. In our ignorance we have limited our peripheries; we have built fences around ourselves and around our Earth. In so doing we have limited ourselves. Today, we cannot escape through the negative door without blasting ourselves into Eternity, but friends from afar are trying to show us a way to escape; a way that can lift us to a transcendent paradise.

The feverish challenge for space control is on. "Conquer or perish," the old slogan, is parading in a new Easter gown. The UFO has made us dig deeper and reach further. Thousands have been released into a new dimension of thought. More thousands are suddenly aware of a different level of consciousness. Others have been catapulted into the creative world where all things are made new. They have touched the realm where man and nature have merged. Man knows intellectually that he is supposed to be a god dwelling in an envelope of flesh and now, in the rare instance, the godship is upon him.

At the core of our being is the pattern of the past, the kernel of the present and the seeds of the future. There is a negative side and a positive side. The one is the essence of experiences that have been lived. The other is a product of the will. Both sides are bound up in the ropes of Earth. The psychic footprints left on the sands of time are there to be read by those who come after. A record is kept whether for good or for evil. If psychic rubbish such as is cluttering our earth today is left; it, too, is an inheritance. This is the negative side.

The pendulum swings again. Man decides he wants no further part in the mess he has created. Everything in him is demanding change. But his dynamic will knows only one way to get the job done. He must fight—fight to the last ditch if necessary. Conquest is the keynote and with a Napoleanic ruthlessness he walks over the dead. Life becomes a bloody melee with nothing to do but continue fighting. This is the positive side.

Neither extreme is the desirable one.

Through the center of these opposites runs the white line of evolution. There are always new frontiers, new points of conquest, new fights and new fighters to be endured. But when they become exhausted with struggle, they sink back into the negative. They retire to rest, to regain some measure of strength.

But not for long. They are again awakened from their lethargy by the cannons of battle. So long as mankind clings to the system of related opposites, the pendulum will swing first to one side, then the other.

It would seem that today we have squeezed the last drop of juice from both these lemons. How can we alter the pattern of these fixations? There is always an answer if we are willing to reconnoiter the unknown; if we are ready to get off the merry-go-round. Since the 1880s millions have dabbled with the psychic sciences. Thousands have a finger in the flying saucer pie. The psychic sciences were a stepping stone to take us out and beyond. But this time we must rise by our own devices into something more than theory. For theory must become a living reality.

Those who have been through these strange experiences incumbent upon the UFO cycle cannot properly transfer the essence of their findings to someone else. There are no adequate words in the vocabulary to describe these happenings. To attempt to relate an experience describing in vivid detail the merger of polarities, the true linking of one plane with another, falls hopelessly short in the telling. Time and the experiences themselves will lay the foundation for a proper glossary—a set of new words that will carry us into the next dimension. When these new dimension levels can be properly charted, then all will begin to comprehend the experiences of the few. They too will know the meaning of "plusage" in earthly experience.

First, we must accept the hypothetical boundary lines. We must accept on faith that there is a balanced interchange between all life, and that all life comes from the One Life. An objective-subjective relationship runs through all things, and as we correlate one idea with another we see this relationship. It begins to make the best kind of sense. Once we have been immersed in that inner certainty there are no more cantankerous doubts. We know it is true because it becomes a living part of us.

There is a saying that "truth is stranger than fiction." We must learn to know truth, bizarre as it seems. "And these signs shall follow them that believe." Whether we accept it or not, this is the very root and fiber of our Christian teachings. Jesus said we could perform as He performed. It seems apparent to us now that He mastered the art of balancing the negative and the positive at center. This means He was able to stir inertia and to tone down violence. Most important, He was then able to find the peace that flows in the middle stream. This is the course we must undertake to master. To combat violence with violence; to match inertia with inertia concentrates the poisons into vile debris. This seems the only way to combat the evils of our time.

The gong pounds in our ears today. The human race is being forced to adapt to a diet of poisons. The soil, the very productivity of life, is poisoned before the tiny seeds have had time to push into the light. Human bodies are plugged with serums made from more horrid substances. The naturalists scream:"Let us go back to the old ways." But is this truly the answer? It would mean regressing into the negative swing. We had epidemics and fevers then as nature burned up the poisons. If we possessed the eye-frequency with which to see it, our earth would present a horrible picture. We would be able to see our atmosphere literally teeming with flotsam, the scum and pollution let loose through radiation from heavy layers of "thought stuff" and other debris, the exudation of hates, fears and lusts held in solution by the weight of gravity. With wars and violence continually on the rampage these vile exudations have burst out of control. The time has come when our bodies must adapt to these lethal substances, or we must give up the fleshy structure in death. We have matched inertia with inertia. We have fought violence with more violence. We have gone along with each swing of the pendulum. But we have never sought the middle stream of peace. Why, then, must we simply return to the old ways, as the naturalists would have us do ?

Where and how did these powers of violence and inertia gain supremacy? Everything leaves behind its ashes—a sediment. Decayed matter goes back to primordial substance. The seed of a flower produces another flower, but decay must precede new growth. The stinkweed produces another stinkweed. One evil thought will carry the radiation of evil for an indefinite time. This residue must be carried over into the next round of existence. Through every department of life this goes on. Pattern is the active principle. Each level of life breeds its like and kind. When the pattern roots are tangled and gnarled we find warped threads throughout the fabric of life. The terminal end of all things begins with the seed. The final manifestation is compounded from the whole. If the residue is good, it produces good. If it is evil, it produces evil.

The pattern behind all manifestation is invisible. Unfortunately, we are a people conditioned to reject that which we cannot see; to accept only that which can be based on so-called fact. But what are the facts? They are results, not principles. Facts alone cannot be classified as reality. Questioning, digging deeper and deeper into the subsoil to find the basis of fact affords a true picture of reality. It was this, the existence of a few isolated facts that brought us to the door of the Space Age. And, of course, to the majority the thought of unoccupied space means capture it, conquer it, gain dominion over it. Take it by force, by violence, by atom bombs—but take it!

How will we react should we discover that space beings have long since abandoned violence as a means of attainment ? What if our bombs and our bullets were to come up against something with the power to resist them? What opposing force could we use against such powerful alchemy? Would we still be arrogant enough to fight blindly on, or would we bow our heads, ashamed of our barbarism? Would we be able to say truthfully, "We're sorry, brothers. We are just ignorant children from Earth."

If we can do this in true humility, then perhaps there is some hope for us. If we can do as they do, we will have scored another point. But if we insist in wallowing in our own foul filth, if we try to argue from our own warped point of view, then what? At heart we are as clean as the best of them. Faced with reality a few might try to cling to their stubborn fixations, but I'll venture the majority will be ready to vote for a change. When a sick man is brought face to face with health, he wants to be healthy himself. He is ready to rise from the couch of his sickness and partake of the puretics. When he can view his horizon with a clean perspective, he too will want to be clean.

What is health? Is a man healthy when he can take rocks into his stomach and digest them? Is he rich when his bank account runs into staggering figures? A stomach built like a fortress can be invaded by cancer. It can still house lethal parasites. The same holds true with a staggering bank account. A full swing of the pendulum and a very rich man can be rendered penniless overnight. It is all part of the pattern of violence we have created.

With Russia racing ahead scientifically the cry is: "Give us more scientists." But are we seeking scientists who can bring us a permanent peace? Or are we looking for men to build bigger and angrier bombs? If we need more scientists, from what bracket of human genius are they to be drawn? Today the people know as much as the master. If science is to grow, if we are going to breed a batch of new scientists they must know where they are going and why. If the men of knowledge we breed will be bent on following the old worn out pattern, if they will lead us into further destruction, then let us think carefully before spending our energies in their creation.

If there are leaders in the ranks of the unsung who can bring us to some new and unexplored paradise, let them come forth. Very recently such a scientist has come forth, not daringly perhaps, because his message is concealed in the folds of fiction. But regardless of form, this book is immensely important. And, unhappily, one of the greatest books of our time will go begging intelligent readers because few on the planet today have advanced to its point of understanding. "The Amazing Mr. Lutterworth" by England's Desmond Leslie (published by Allan Wingate, London) is a must on the list of every advanced thinker. Here is perhaps one of the truest stories of the space people ever told. Only one who has made space contact either by "channeling" or otherwise could have written such a book. Only one dedicated to the greatest cause in history would have dared to write it.

It is apparent to all that our universal batteries have run down. The healthiest and wisest of Earthlings have not found a panacea for our inadequacies. Our civilization is going through a torturous travail and we are the victims.

What about cataclysm? Would this wipe the slate clean? Would it give us the new start we are seeking? The question is: Do we want cataclysm, or do we want a miracle? Jesus told us we could perform the same miracles He performed. In a footnote to the book "A Dweller on Two Planets," Phylos the Tibetan said : "One will come after me who will tell thee more of the Great Deep of Life than I. Await her words." I sincerely believe this one is none other than Diane, who calls herself a Venusian. She has shown us the way to miracles by way of tapping the creative essence at Source. Is she one of the miracle makers come to show us the way ?

The potentiality for the great miracle lies dormant within us all. When we are willing to abandon the rubbish we will be led by unseen hands. We will receive the inspiration to guide us. One who is spurred on by the spirit of adventure is not daunted by appearances. We have conquered the material strongholds. Now we are out to conquer space with identical weapons. We are not trying to speculate on what we might find a million miles up. We're taking it for granted we will find another Earth.

To soar away into space unprepared might set the clock back many centuries. There will be volunteers. There will be casualties. But wouldn't it be wiser to learn something about the new dimension before we attempt to enter that dimension? The most intrepid of explorers tries to learn all he can before he sets out on his journey. Can we depend upon the sputnik and our own space devices to chart the unknown for us? Wouldn't it be safer to train human sensitives, those who know how to reel out the lifeline into the unknown? Would the end result be worth the try?

We are none of us satisfied with today's pseudo-freedoms. If we are going to find universal freedom we must begin to face facts. The weight of adverse resistance must be lifted so that when we can see through, we can break through. The Pilgrim Fathers risked their all in search for religious freedom. The explorer risks his life in search of new lands. The strong-willed and the fearless have done the trail-blazing. Through it all life has been a saga in the quest for freedom.

In our religion the orthodox point of view represents the negative side—man too infantile to handle his own inadequacies must have a Scapegoat, a personal Savior. There must be something or someone to absolve his weaknesses—someone to bless and care for him.

The heterodox take the positive side. They tend to accentuate the positive and ignore the negative. "No problem will go away because its feelings are hurt at being ignored." We cannot hope to escape by adopting the ostrich complex. We cannot stick our heads in the sand and wish the thing would go away. Both the positive or the negative by themselves throw the scales off-balance; an imbalance that must sometime be made manifest in planetary life itself.

The negative is the feminine—the life-giver. The positive is the masculine-the penetrating force. The negative, or feminine, holds the seeds of the race in solution. When man asserts his positive side the human ego is born. Out of it comes the psychic octopus of greed and aggression. The wholly positive individual knows no law but to trample beneath his feet his more docile brother. It is here that world aggression begins. From this seed the dictator is born. The positive and negative relationship runs through all things, but unless there is a balance between the objective and the subjective there can be no underlying unity. Balance is necessary to keep us from becoming one sided. If we are to know harmony in life, there must be a perfect interchange between negative and positive; between inner and outer. Until such time as we do have correlation we shall not know the meaning of true universalism. The positive and negative must be blended, and they must be blended at center.

CHAPTER FIVE

There burns within each and every one of us an incandescent light that can never be extinguished. It may lower to a flicker throughout a lifespan; there may be times when it has seemingly blacked out altogether, but there always comes a day when it is again fanned into a luminous flame.

When we trace the lifeline of those dedicated to a cosmic task we usually find they have experienced these fires of illumination. They have known, if but for a few moments, that complete Oneness. Their knowledge has not grown from books, but from a flowering within themselves.

Such a time came for me in 1939. It was a day of gathering up the waste and debris and casting it into the eternal flame. I quote from my book, "Flight to Venus":

"My body became alive with a peculiar tingling glow. In an instant the feeling permeated every cell and atom of my being. It seemed to be dancing to the ecstasy of strange, polarized currents. The door to my mind opening and closing caused my consciousness to swing back and forth between reality and unreality.

"I leaped to my feet as if to herald in some cosmic drama. Then IT came, straining at my ankles like a gorgeous display of lighted fireworks; a transcendent violet flame that fanned out until it enveloped my body like an aura of sacred fire. As the flames grew in intensity, extending over a wide periphery, the flame raced through every cell, cleansing and purifying as it went. Channels of my mind that had been tightly closed before, opened up like an enchanted lotus flower. I was vibrant, magnetic, and I could feel the effervescence of an enthusiasm I had never felt before. My heart beating in rhapsodic rhythm was tuned in now to the heartbeat of the universe. I was no longer a citizen of a little, inhibited world, but a guest in the World Universal. I was no longer a separate entity, a human person, but a part and parcel of every inch of God's glorious creation.

In that moment I knew, as others before have known, the true meaning of the Unity and ONENESS OF ALL.

"The sacred flame grew into a holocaust of splendor, continuing for an indefinite time. It finally died away, leaving only an essence. Alive with the fire of creation, everything within my range of vision had changed. The landscape, the wild flowers, the trees; they fairly scintillated with an array of gorgeous hues. They were not something apart now. I was one with them. They were one with me. In those sacred moments, I came to know the meaning of life. With the opening of the channels of perception, under the living reality of all things I stood with clarity. No longer bound to the bondage of earth, my mind and soul were at last free to travel at will."

I did not know it then, but this was the beginning of my task ahead. I was on the threshold of new vista, but the time had not yet come for me to enter. The laying of the new foundation was an insuperable task. I was ground down to bedrock—the point of new beginnings. I was without the tools and the means of rising by my own bootstraps. The day had not been made ready, for I was ahead of the cosmic calendar. While I had for a few beautiful moments glimpsed the universal housetop, I still had to begin in the basement. It was only as I was forced to rise step by step that I could find the true equations. It seems the human spirit must wander in the bottomless grottos; it must make frequent pilgrimages to its beginnings.

It is never an easy road for it is ever strewn with the thorns and thickets. The thicker the brush the more awareness it requires to go through. Awareness is gained on the file of experience. The bridge between the conscious and the unconscious must be spanned and it must be spanned by human robots.

Recently Prime Minister U Nu of Burma made this statement to the West; "According to the ancient teachings here is but one way which will lead to freedom from suffering. This is none other than the way of complete awareness."

Those who become aware and know the meaning of awareness are often relegated to the realm of the psychotic. Seldom are they recognized in their lifetime, but must wait for posthumous recognition. Nevertheless, they unquestionably represent segments of change. At certain intervals in the history of the world they come out of obscurity to lead the processional. They strike the gong of the cosmic clock. They open the universal reservoirs. Eventually thousands from every bracket of society join in the march. They take on the job of clearing away the debris, the densities created by the blunders of humanity. They set to work with a will to find ways to cleanse the Earth, to rid it of its poisons so that it can start over again.

Is it necessary to sink to the depths in order to rise to the heights? No ! Absolutely not! We can clean the slate without the vicious caprice of the elements; without guns and cannons; without nuclear bombs. But as the lovely Diane once said: "The files of tradition will be closed and the memory of the past will be blotted out. Tradition will be left behind." The Sun is rapidly fading on the horizon today. We have seen the rays of murky light, the density of the Earth's fog. There is still time for accomplishment, but time is growing short. In the closing days of this cycle every department of life will be speeded up. Days and nights of eternity will be condensed in a few brief years. We have been given many reprieves, but the time has come for final decision.

Are we equal to gaining the poise, tolerance and understanding needed to make the transition to a world of fresh creation? Our reaction to the strange mutations we will experience in its unwinding process will measure the time it will require to uncoil toward the upward spiral.

Many are waiting. The very air is splitting with tenseness. A glance at the news headlines is all one needs to know that the world mind is in a horrible muddle. The slaughter of kings and monarchs is part of the brutal picture. When ideals are shattered, when hearts are riddled, the first thought is to avenge a seeming wrong. This has continued so long that there is little real security left anywhere.

The butchery and devastation will eventually come to an abrupt end. Human beings will tire of stepping through blood and gore. One by one they will seek some peaceful citadel where their minds will be at rest and they can think pure thoughts.

Many who have never prayed will fall to their knees in earnest. They will take part in the healing consciousness. They will join the long processional. This will be the time when ships will be seen sailing through the crystalline skies on and on into the interior regions of space. With the awakening, we will look eagerly toward the Space Age and the Brotherhood of Man.

The prospect of this awakening has made many ready and willing to tread the strange paths today. Basic consciousness is needed to prepare the new roadways in the sky. The pioneers of space consciousness will make mistakes, perhaps. They can expect many setbacks, but as they move forward, one day they will know victory. It is a lonely road they travel, for they have only unseen hands and inspiration from On High to guide them.

We are all human magnets. We have the power to draw to us anything we desire. At the points of transition we find the strongest force. This is the middle road where energies are transmuted into the "greater energies;" the newness of all things.

It is a staggering thought, but many believe preparation will be completed within the framework of one generation. We can make of our Earth the greatest commonwealth we have ever known, or we can lapse back into a centuries-long slumber.

Those who have dedicated their lives to change have assurance they will have plenty of assistance. They believe that beings from other planets will come to Earth to help them. Some these other-planetary beings will seek embodiment in Earth bodies. Others will come in ships. Perhaps they will come to show us how to draft the manumission of justice, of peace, of beautiful living. Perhaps they will tell us how the moral fiber of men and nations can be improved. Perhaps they will draft for us a true mandate of brotherly love.

This is the decree of the Light Bearers. If we are willing to follow, eventually we will see the dazzling light. As the darkness begins to fade, intelligence will supplant bigotry and wisdom will rule the Earth.

UP RAINBOW HILL

CHAPTER SIX

The Lord sayeth: "I am the Alpha and Omega, the beginning and the ending, which is and which was and which is to come . . . the ALMIGHTY."

In this quotation we are shown the way into the Space Age. If we believe ourselves to be intelligent, let us act with intelligence. It is reasonable to assume that we cannot cling to the Earth Age and try to reach for the Space Age at the same time. We must abandon one in favor of the other. In the past decade many have experienced this new dimension in consciousness. Their minds have been projected over the threshold where they have witnessed the breakthrough. Unless that consciousness is aborted by a constant flow of negatives, they will be able to breakthrough themselves.

In the meantime some will stumble blindly on, coming up each day with something new. If we use our heads we will know that we cannot tap the reservoirs of space with spades and boring devices. We cannot use the obsolete tools of Earth to dig our way through. We are a long stride from the shoreline of transcendental conceptions, but when we finally reach it we will find many strange fish in that new sea. Lines have been cast many times, but always in a hit-and-miss fashion. We cannot repeat too often that in the past we have lived in our dichotomies—the dualities of existence. The dichotomies must be metamorphosed into trichotomies—a three-dimensional middle of the road. There we will find about which we have so long prayed, but to which we have never gained entrance. Dichotomy is knowing by way of the balanced opposites. Trichotomy is putting those opposites to work as ONE. When we learn how to function in three dimensions, we will be able to ride a spaceship into the New Age.

Perhaps we are not as far away as we think. The genius of science is not confined to the letter of the book. Those who have touched the universal spheres are capable of pure perception. They alone can gather up the essence at each level of consciousness. They can measure the interplay between spirit and matter. Such a man has appeared on our Earth's horizon. His name is Otis T. Carr and he comes from Baltimore, Maryland.

Mr. Carr has been living on this planet for more than fifty years. In his half century of living, the merger has never been broken, but he admits there have been many times when it has been badly strained.

Today it has come to pass that Otis Carr believes he has found the key to the greatest revelation of the ages hidden in the folds of symbolism; the use of God's free energy to run the wheels of the world. Plans are in the making now to pilot his own spaceship powered by God's free energy out into space. Destination—the Moon. Mr. Carr tentatively set December 7, 1959 as the date for the flight. This marks the fifty-fifth year on Earth of this man, who has experienced the ONENESS with ALL; the man who has projected his vision into the far horizons is now ready to take his body along for companionship.

His first "illumination" came at the tender age of five years. He tells how he was born at the edge of the woods near Elkins, West Virginia; how nature was his first playmate. This little boy, alone most of the time, learned to love every leaf and petal with tender affection. Birds took little morsels of food from his baby hands. They sang for him in the dawning light. The wild flowers conversed with him. Even the wicked stinger of the bee and the wasp held no fear for this child of nature. He loved them all for God had made them all.

Otis Carr remembers his first breakthrough as though it happened yesterday. He had wandered through the woods following an electrical storm. He stood fascinated, watching two little raindrops hanging from an oak leaf. He immediately designated one he, the other she. Something deep in his consciousness told him that they were twin-souls that had started back in the night of time. It told him that someday they would grow up to become ONE SOUL. They would be separated through millions of years, perhaps. But one day they would be reunited. Each complement would find its ONE-NESS close to the throne of God.

At the age of five, the soul of this little man-child merged with the Soul of Nature. It was then that Otis T. Carr learned that all planes of existence are linked with the Universal Soul.

That Earthman has within him the same potential as the gods. That he has the capacity to touch and tap the solar elements whereby the planetary gates can be opened. At the age of five, when the abandoned the old to take on the new, this little boy was able to flow with the universal tides. He learned the meaning of universal seership and the intuitive completeness between the visible and invisible. He was henceforth to be aware of an absolute relativity between the planes of earth and the farthest star.

The second breakthrough came as substantiation of his childhood experience. A voice out of nowhere counseled him:

"At the tender age of five years, in December, the month of your nativity, in the year nineteen hundred and nine, on a mountainside in Western Virginia, was revealed to you a magnificent sight: a cross over the full moon expanding throughout the heavens with rays brilliant and purer than spun gold. As thy later knowledge about this science has confirmed, it was no trick of the optics. It was decreed by the Cosmic that thou should be the modern witness to His sign in the Heavens."

The third break-through came in the nature of a mystical revelation when the mystery of The Sphinx was shown to him. Again he heard the voice out of the voiceless spheres:

"Earth Child, thou who was chosen by the Cosmic at the turn of the century for a particular task, harken well and listen attentively to thy third cosmic revelation from space. At long last the full meaning of thy previous revelations is known to thee, and the great wonderment of this new knowledge fills thy heart and mind, but fear and concern have departed and thy mind has proved worthy of this new cosmic illumination."

To quote Otis Carr on this: "It was then I came into the full realization of the significance of the fourth division of a concentric curve and the sixth geometric division of the sphere. Without recourse to textbook research or search into the archives of arcane or esoteric wisdom, I knew that the equilateral triangle held within its form the dimensions of the story of creation."

Then the voice out of nowhere continued: "You know for yourself that the motion and velocity of the Planet Earth could be dimensionally duplicated in a relative measure and equation, and that the energies involved could thereby be made manifest. You designed and made a small device, a reflecting prism that demonstrated how vibratory energy could be returned to its source."

This sounds like a parable to all who have taken on a greater degree of materiality than they can handle. But is this not what we have been seeking since time immemorial? Has this man, whose heart is as big as a mountain, the smile on his lips the reflection of his soul, actually found the medium to change the cloak of the world?

That it should come at the exact moment in time when the shift of the cycles is imminent seems more than mere coincidence. Is this part of the deus ex machina that will devour our ills and give us that fresh start? When the debris is cleared from the road, then we can enter that transcendental spectrum and start our climb up Rainbow Hill. At the summit we swill find the vista of new reality.

There ere no accidents in nature. All things are timed with precision accuracy. Nothing is chance-sprung. All of this added together, it would seem that Otis T. Carr is a man of destiny. Going back with him into his teenage span, this young man had another overwhelming desire. He wanted to transfer to canvas some of nature's beautiful patterns that had been etched on his soul. The time came when he went to New York to study art. He had no money to support himself, but this did not stop him. He soon got a job as a package room clerk in a large downtown hotel. One day a tall, emaciated stranger stopped at his desk.

"Young man," he said, "when you have finished here, please bring four pounds of unsalted peanuts to my suite." That man today is enjoying posthumous fame. He was the great scientist and nature lover, Nikola Tesla. The peanuts were to feed his pigeons, for Tesla loved birds with the passion of St. Francis.

It was that day in 1925 that Otis T. Carr's trip to the Moon began. Almost daily he sat a neophyte at the feet of his master. It was here his destiny was to begin its long trek to fruition. In a few years he would be experimenting with free energy as fuel for automobiles, aircraft, oceanliners, trains, factory machines of all kinds, lighting entire cities, and perhaps, in time, furnishing the very food that builds and sustains our bodies.

The outward manifestation of those days in the fabulous 20s is now nearing the finish line. Today a gigantic plan is under way to create a new city completely powered by free energy. This greatest of all ventures to come in our cycle will cover a large tract of land eighteen miles from Baltimore, Maryland, where the Space Research Institute will be built. It will be the center for the production of free energy prototype applications. As these prototypes are perfected they will be licensed for use by manufacturers who will apply them to produce products already familiar to the public. The first use of the Carr free energy devices will be in the building complex of Space Institute itself. The buildings will be completely powered, lighted and mechanized by the free energy space forces of gravity and magnetism. The Institute will be surrounded by a model community, including a large spaceport for the landing of visiting crafts, hotels, residences and complete shopping facilities for thousands of employees, their families, and guests from all parts of the Solar System. Here will be fabricated the first forty-five-foot spacecraft which Mr. Carr plans to pilot to the Moon and back.

Otis Carr sat at the feet of the Great Tesla for three long years. He knew then this unusual man might have changed the momentum of the world and advanced global civilization more than a thousand years, had his greatest of all creations not been suppressed because it would have upset our well-grooved economy. But Tesla left one device that cannot be suppressed—the flaming guidepost for his young disciple: "If you are to understand the inventions of Tesla," he said, "you must first attune your mind to God."

Otis Carr speaks freely about tapping the universal forces through his free energy devices. He will tell you that his textbook is the Bible. When Jesus said: "Before Abraham was I AM," he expressed the ABSOLUTE. All who have known illumination, if only a mere flash, know the meaning of touching the ABSOLUTE.

"The Universe has two basic properties," says Carr. "The motions and the directions. The correlation of these properties manifest in several forms; their two categories being energy and matter. These two forms are equal to each other, and are the product of each other, matter being under the pressure of motion, and having relative finity because of the harmonious correlation of the direction of such pressure, and energy being matter released from pressure by any change in the direction of motion.

"In any universal system, these motions and directions manifest their finite totality in what we call space, and describe their total form in what we call straight lines and curves, the geometry of which is expressed in a finite form whose dimensions are a constant correlation of the directions and motions. l have equated the shape of this universal space and translated it into physical form which we have called the Utron Electrical Accumulator, which expresses the linear correlation of space motions and directions in a form that is therefore completely round and completely square.

"In its linear proportions the Utron Electrical Accumulator is the union of straight lines brought together in and from all directions, and in its correlation of and with curved lines, it expands from a point to the circumference of its equator, and contracts from that equator to a point, always being a correlation of complete curves. The sum of these linear dimensions is three points, the exact centerpoint of which +0=-0, and the exact peripheral points of which are +X and -X.

$$-0/0 = x/+x \quad 0 +X = 0X$$

Otis Carr says:

"One important aspect of this development is that when it is used to power a spacecraft, there is no so-called "blasting off," The OTC-X1 will float off the earth, will be self-regenerating, will be wrapped in its own electromagnetic field with complete protection from radiation, heat, weightlessness and other problems that hamper ordinary space-flight thinking."

He explains that free energy, as he uses the phrase, describes the perpetual forces of gravity and electromagnetism that are every where at work in the universe. Unlike conventional, manufactured power, these forces cannot be "used up" and they are free for the taking. Until now the problem has been how to take them and put them to work for man. He believes the problem has been solved by using an interplay of gravity and electromagnetism in a delicate balance of enormous potential power.

When Otis Carr first asked Mother Nature to reveal her secrets he was led to the symbol of the Cross. Here he found the answer to equation. Following his training with Tesla he delved backward traditionally into the teachings of the ancients, then forward to the moderns, including Einstein and Steinmetz.

He will tell you that he starts from the God-principle working downward, and with the Earth principle working upward. He has experienced this ONENESS in his own life, therefore he is able to correlate it on a universal scale.

Tesla worked on the identical principle. In the year 1899 he experimented with a device he hoped would supply free energy to every point on the planet. His plan would have enabled the world to tap this energy just as we now tune in radio and television. It is well understood why he had no encouragement in the creation of such a device. It would have utterly crippled the Edison setup.

Tesla inventions ran into the hundreds. He gave the world the alternating current generator, its motor and electrical transmission systems. Nikola Tesla's creations provide the very base of our ignition and broadcasting systems of today. Yet he died in poverty and disillusionment in a small cheap hotel in New York. And we the people of America must carry this scar on our souls forever. He left little for those who came after to inherit, for he built most of his creations in his mind, seldom transferring them to paper. Now more than a decade after his death we are trying to piece together the fragments of his greatness. But how are we going to solve these difficult mathematical problems in his head? How can we command the elements to do our bidding? When we trace the long red line of great souls on earth we find few of them have left written records for posterity. But there has always been someone to whom they have communicated their secrets before death. Was Otis Carr the one to whom the great Nikola Tesla entrusted his cryptic messages? Or could it be the electrical genius of our time is at present whispering into the ear of Otis Carr from some peaceful point beyond the veil?

Tesla was years ahead of his time. He was a way-paver. Since World War II the pace of the world has been speeded up. The splitting of the atom has brought us to a point of crisis. It is apparent that a man of Nikola Tesla's stature did not discover his creations by himself. He was merely the channel through which they flowed. True channelship is passed on from one to the next. Otis Carr would have been a logical one to inherit this channelship, or at least to inherit the potential to be developed within himself. But this would not prevent the overshadowing influence of the Tesla soul.

It is hoped that Otis Carr has come to us in time to save us from our own murderous hands. The balloon will not hold another patch. Even kings will be dethroned when the gas bag collapses over their heads. We must look skyward for support. The octopus of greed must be slain with our own arrows. The false gods we have created must be sent back to the grottos and the subworlds. The gap from these grottos has grown wider and wider. The demons are ever ready to seduce us.

We cannot change the unchanging face of time, but we can change that which enters into the periphery of time. The masses are in subconscious revolt. They are demanding change. They want nothing further to do with mirages. It must be something tangible this time; something they can place their faith in and cling to.

The voices peaking to Otis Carr from beyond said:

"Have patience; listen carefully. The hands of time turn backward. Three million-six-hundred-fifty-thousand turns of the Earth past, and ten thousand journeys of velocity in its path around the Sun, the spot and vicinity where thee now stand was a paradise on Earth. God was indeed proud of His creations."

Power-seeking man knows nothing of brotherly love. We can only know this love when the monster GREED has been slain. It is hard to slay the alien while man still loves his rotting civilization. But one day he will crawl into the grave with the sleeping dead. He will meet the wrathful deities to whom he has given his allegiance. He will then know that he alone has been the author of his present ills. Steeped in patterns of violence, he has withered at his own roots. He will know too that his aggression is at the heart of his evils.

Today blind leaders are leading the blind. Most of them have gone "atom-mad." Is this the way we must forfeit our best efforts? Must we fall at the feet of false gods and their nefarious schemes? Must all governments crumble before we are ready to face the lamentable truth?

Chaos is on a rampage. We are captives held in self-inflicted bondage. Each cycle of violence makes a wider gap, puts us just that much farther away from home base; still farther away from the House of God.

That which is new must lead the way even if those who lead us must be ridiculed. If they are strong somewhere they will find Job's patience, the fortitude of the greats who have gone before.

In the end the emergence of the new order is inevitable. For the path ahead we must look to the way-showers. Nikola Tesla was one of these men. Perhaps Otis Carr is another. His head has been on the chopping block just as the UFO sighters have been through the scourge. Many are ready to lend a helping hand. This is not a cult. It is a crusade. It is the measurement of the far-reaching changes that must come to our Earth.

At this stage no one can accurately foretell the extent of the Carr experiments, but to one who has had expansion of consciousness the principle is sound. And if the principle is basic, the results to follow should be all that is expected.

Otis Carr learned about free energy by studying the laws of the universe; laws that can only be learned through direct perception. The orthodox scientist who has gained his knowledge through study and classification of phenomena would not understand this method. When one has learned to function, if only momentarily, in his higher bodies, he can then view the universe at a glance. Otis Carr believes that all bodies must mesh in unison, that the electronic field must be brought into play as an individual force field before Earthman will dare to venture into space.

Otis Carr knows the meaning of the Universal Absolute. He knows that each infinitesimal part of the universe is dependent upon the others. When one has touched the realm of conscious immortality, his conscious awareness can penetrate all forms, for he is ONE with them all.

"Poverty is the scourge of our planet. It breeds filth and debris and is the parent of crime," says Mr. Carr. Is free energy the medium through which the world will know economic security? Otis Carr believes that it is. Free energy holds none of the dangers of a war-built prosperity. It has no circumference; no limitations. With it there would be no further need to cling to things and ideas that have lost their usefulness. We would be constantly striving for new levels, not new things. This is the way we can soar into space with the Planet Earth our spaceship.

CHAPTER SEVEN

Is this the message the UFOs have for us? Since the days of the first sightings people the world over have been clamoring for more knowledge. Out of the ranks of the enthusiasts many will volunteer to serve the social and economic developments ahead. Others will dedicate themselves to trying to raise the vibrational level of the human family.

I recall my first visit to the fabulous Giant Rock in 1954. It was inspired wholly by curiosity, but I was soon pondering the reason thousands had wound their way over the sandy terrain to listen to fairy tales. Further curiosity stimulated me to gather with the crowd and ask questions. When I engaged them in conversation it was my turn to have a red face. The stories they told amazed me. Sightings over the rock were a common occurrence. These people were sincerely interested in the changes they hoped might come. "We're seeking a better world to live in," some of them told me. "If the space people can show us a better way we're on their side," others chimed in. And so it went. They were all tired of the dichotomous grind; one day seemingly secure, the next day with all their security knocked from under them.

Since that time literally hundreds of groups have sprung up all over the world; little concentrations of people have banded together for a specific purpose—they want to know more. They want to be a part of this new thing. They are willing to help in any way they can to bring a new Earth into being. There is an idealistic beat in the breast of every one of them. They're gambling with stardust, to be sure. And occasionally one goes off the deep end, but they are going off the deep end in other camps, too. How deep can the atom bomb go?

The consciousness behind the so-called reality has built the reality. Little do the ignorant realize the immeasurable good these little innocent groups have done in contributing to that consciousness. Filled and running over with strange soul ardor, they no longer look to things Earthly for the answers, but rather to the founts of wisdom in the highest ethers. They have their leaders, too; leaders perhaps as frail as their followers.

But at least they have stepped out of the foul mass and are trying to wipe away the slime.

The spark has been ignited. Little by little they are adding knowledge to the relationship between all life, everywhere. There is no vanity in them; they have no personal ambitions. They no longer believe that this one little Earth is the single important planet in the universe. They're not sure what they will find when they reach other planets, whether sub-humans or super-humans, but they know that we are all subconsciously tied together on the same invisible cord. All possess hearts and souls because God made them that way. All are enthroned somewhere in a greater divine consciousness. By means of growth they hope to reach it, touch it, embrace it.

The grand processional is marching. Those who have joined the parade must get to their destination, and they'll keep marching until their last days on earth.

The masses are waiting and anxious. Many of the scoffers, despite their armor-plate fixations, are beginning to feel the chrysalis burst. They have moments when they shudder with some inner foreboding. The chart, with its trends and its tendencies, is there to be read. It requires little human intelligence to know that old things have lost their ability to serve; that we are living in days of crisis. "For as the new Heaven and the new Earth which I shall make shall remain before me," sayeth the Lord. "And it shall come to pass that from one new Moon to another, and from one Sabbath to another, shall all flesh come to worship before me." (Isaiah 6622-23).

Brotherhood is not an alien word to many of us. Today millions the world over carry the blood of another fellow-being in his veins. An hour, a day or an epoch is only as large as the consciousness that sustains it. We've taken the low road, and there have been times when we have tried to reach the high road. The time has come to take the road between.

Diane has said: "The center of gravity has been called by your wise ones, the seat of intelligence. It is here that gravity and levity meet and static is transformed into energy. This is the tonal center where individual chords vibrate with universal chords. It is likewise the gateway through which the vital energies from the outer areas of space can flow."

One day we will wake up to the great changes that have come since 1947, the year of the UFO. It has been a chaotic breakthrough, and that which has been broken up must inevitably leave behind its crumbling debris. Confusion is on the ascendancy. There can be no cooperation with those who refuse to open their eyes and their minds. Antipathy has put vitriol on their tongues, ignorance in their souls.

We cannot play at the game with both ends of the stick. We cannot view these strange phenomena wholly through Earthly binoculars and still find the right answers. To ignore the possibility of vast stages of advancement is to sell ourselves short. What others have done we can do also. To deny that possibility is to attempt to stifle our own advancing cycle.

It might seem like a long jump from one octave to another. But haven't we been slowly evolving one note at a time all along? If our next step is to be an age immeasurably advanced over our present stage, how can we accurately measure it by our way of life?

If we can believe the seers and the mystics, the planet Venus is our elder sister. My own other-dimensional experience goes back to the year 1939 and my purification in the orchid-magenta flame. My twin body went through the necessary change and I was transported, or rather teleported, to the Planet of Love. It was an experience that will remain etched on my consciousness forever. Furthermore, it has given me a working premise; something by which I can partially explain the meaning of the advanced octave. We live and move and have our being in a three-dimensional world. Millions on, our planet have not yet advanced to three-dimensional thinking. A few have gone on ahead, and in some vague way have experienced the overshadowing of a fourth dimension. The fourth dimension furnishes a pattern for the first, second and third dimension. In the long cycle we have just endured, the fourth dimension has been completely abstract. We could dream about it but with our limited vision we could not see it. Nevertheless, the fourth dimension might be likened to a seed pushing up through the darkened soil. The masters and adepts have told us that one day we shall inherit the fourth dimension not as an invisible pattern, but as a complete and tangible plane, the ground of the New Age. Briefly put, the abstract world will become concrete.

Stated another way, our Earth is three-dimensional, overshadowed by an abstraction we call fourth dimension. If venus is our higher "arc;" that is to say, a complete octave higher in the scale of evolution, the fourth dimension of Earth would be the first dimension of Venus. By the same token, Venusians have grasped a dimension which roughly corresponds to our fourth. They have conquered the intricacies of the seventh dimension.

Many advanced beings live on the planet Earth, many who possess extrasensory powers. Using their subtle bodies as a means of projection, they can travel through space with the ease of a bird. Many have been able to go into long periods of catalepsy, their bodies seemingly lifeless. Yet they were alive with a vitality the ordinary human knows nothing about.

It is apparent that their magical feats are accomplished by means of fourth-dimensional powers. If our fourth dimension is paralleled by the first dimension of Venus, how can we hope to measure the powers of those who have touched a seventh level? What sort of extraterrestrial magic might we expect from them ? How can we expect to measure another dimension on our inadequate yardstick?

Each new perspective leads to new discoveries. The human mind can reach out to touch the unknown and unseen worlds, and that touch can be uncannily accurate. There are countless numbers of sensitive individuals capable of this touch with us today. It is their job to pave the groundwork of the future. Call them what we will: mystics, seers or just dreamer; if they can perceive the beyond, they can discover the beyond.

Our world religions have not yet reached this point.

Our scientists reject that which they cannot perceive.

Many shrug their shoulders as if to ward off a blow. Never before have we stewed in our own lethal poisons as we are stewing today. People are no longer satisfied to let a chicken grow old. The poor barnyard fowl scarcely has time to grow up before the axe is at its throat. Speed! We're wound up like spinning tops racing off to nowhere. Perhaps we would not be so enthusiastic if our own lives were cut in half because of our speed.

We are told there is a stepped-up bombardment of cosmic rays. This should spell something by way of proving that our solar system is racing into new areas of space. Perhaps there has never been a precedent to our present-day state of affairs. Doesn't the evidence speak for itself? The time has come when the shadows are becoming the realities. The smashing of the atom was man's last gigantic achievement. Now we must face the facts. The date of the start on the long material descent may one day be measured from the beginning of the Atomic Age. Since the atom represents the "negative phase" it will help us race downward, but it will not aid in our ascendancy.

If we can sensitize our bodies and our minds to rise to meet those who are already functioning from the higher vibration, then why not set out in earnest? If it is true that we have visitors from other planets they have had plenty of time to prove whether they are friends or foes. So far, there is no evidence that they are here to destroy us.

Speeding up in a constructive sense means getting closer to the borderline of change. This is evidenced by ever-occurring new experiences. Until we find an outlet, a way through to that land of paradise, we will naturally be burned in our own flames.

What is the first lesson we must learn? Perhaps it is the use and adaptation of the true Creative Substance, something man has sought for unconsciously, but never found except in substitution. The teachings of Diane might help to bring us closer to that reality. I quote from "Over The Threshold": "Throughout the centuries, in the twinkling of an eye, has baffled earthman because he knows nothing of the transmutative powers of the universe. He has never fully understood the Christ concept. He does not know the meaning of instantaneous manifestation because it is contrary to the known laws of earth.

"Earthman accepts prayer as seeking the intervention of the Divine. He does not know that when prayers are singularly answered, he has by accident, touched the laws of transmutation. When thought or strong desire is sent out to God in true faith, the prayerful one has touched the Soul of the Essene—the essence. The answer is forthcoming by way of revelation for the Creative Substance is made manifest in the form of desire."

When this creative essence is harnessed and brought to use, then all things can be accomplished "in the twinkling of an eye." They will be accomplished in a constructive way. Jesus changed the vibrations of His body. He walked on the waters. He could make himself invisible at will. He could rid his body of death-laden cells, replacing them with vital, health-giving plasmas. Again I quote from "Over The Threshold":

"When the Master Jesus left your earth," says Diane, "He left behind His Spirit, for his Spirit is Divine Essence. He released a flow of this essence which has sustained your earth to this day. At His passing a holocaust of spiritual flame spread over the earth gathering up the poisons of evil and transmuting them."

Why has science failed to discover this mysterious essence? Perhaps because we would have tried to adapt it to the war machine. We would be sure to apply it to further ways of destruction. It is a simple principle that is involved; so simple, in fact, that we have failed to find the key. When matter is reduced to its smallest particle, the frequency that motivates matter is still intact. Matter is reduced to vibration. As vibration it can be utilized in the manner Otis Carr has made clear.

In teleportation, bodies are transported through space by dissolving the atoms at one point and reassembling them according to the identical pattern at another. Many know this can be done, but no one as yet has been able to demonstrate the technique under laboratory conditions.

Jesus said: "He that believeth in me, the works that I do shall he do also; and greater works than these shall he do."

Creative ESSENCE is the basis of all things: "Seek ye first the Kingdom of Heaven." That is, seek for the first substance and all other things will be added for the first substance is the primary of all things.

CHAPTER EIGHT

Every great event leaves its mark on the tablets of time. Miracles are always with us. But when a miracle is explained it is no longer a miracle. Digging into the tomes of knowledge that have long since gathered dust, we find plenty of evidence that spaceships are not new; that they have been coming through the centuries.

There can be no doubt, then, that the ships have been coming to our skies, and the factual evidence we are seeking seems to match up. If space ships have been seen, is it irrational to believe they contained space men?

Where is the proof? Tangible evidence is not, of course, readily available. Only calculations of length, breadth and thickness are acceptable to the materialist. But, whether we accept it or not, truth can be drawn from varying levels of experience. It is an established fact that truth coming from the subtle realms is often the most intense form of truth, for it is much closer to its creator.

The January-February 1957 issue of "Flying Saucer Review" (London) daringly ran an article by M. Alexander titled, "UFOs Seen By Sixty Thousand Witnesses." Here are a few excerpts from the article:

"Nearly all contemporary readers are well aware of the many incidents recorded in the Bible that bear an almost exact relationship to present-day recordings of UFOs. But how many are aware of the greatness of all recordings? A recording that no one can dispute, for the facts are there, word for word, of an actual landing and appearance—be it objective or subjective. I refer here to "Our Lady of Fatima."

"On October 13, 1917, a pouring wet day, between 60 and 70 thousand people of all classes, believers and unbelievers alike, went to the Cova da Iria with the children. Atheists and mockers were among the crowd, together with journalists sent from Lisbon to represent the leading Portuguese newspapers.

"There, suddenly, at 2 p.m., the crowd saw what appeared to be the Sun coming down through the clouds. It rotated three times for about four minutes each time, various coloured lights and intense heat, although it was not too bright for the people to gaze directly at it. Some described it afterward as a silvery disc. After about twelve minutes the disc appeared to move back to its normal place in the sky, where it resumed its usual brilliance so that people could no longer took directly at it."

Another extract states:

"At Fatima, on October 13, 1917, the day was wet and dull. The Sun had not appeared all morning, and the people who went there stood in the pouring rain. At 2 p.m. the thousands of people present, or at least the vast majority of them, saw the clouds part, showing the clear blue sky beyond them. They looked up and the Sun appeared like a pale disc, not dazzling at all. One woman present said it looked like steel. Others said rather like silver; others again like mother-of-pearl. All agreed it was no strain at all upon the eyes to look at it.

"Suddenly the pale disc appeared to detach itself from the sky, come down through the break in the clouds, and go through an extraordinary series of movements, radiating the most variously colored beams of light, three separate times of four minutes each."

In a letter dated December 15, 1949, Harley Wood, government astronomer of New South Wales, Australia, wrote in response to a request:

"I have no record of any astronomical event which would fit the description you give. It sounds rather like a highly fanciful description of a total eclipse of the Sun, but there was no eclipse of the sun in that year (1917).

"The only reasonable conclusion is that whatever happened at Fatima, we must rule out any merely natural explanation of it as a total eclipse of the sun. It in no way proves that the events reported at Fatima did not occur. As a matter of fact, had the astronomers recorded a total eclipse of the sun on that day, it would play right into the hands of the unbelievers who would have said that Between 60 and 70 thousand fools had mistaken an ordinary eclipse for a miraculous heavenly manifestation. Skeptics therefore, are at least robbed of that explanation..."

He says further: "It is certain that on October 13, 1917, the actual sun in no way altered its position in relation to this earth. It did not leave its place in the sky, travel the 93,000,000 miles to this earth, and come through the clouds at Fatima, in order to manifest itself to the 60 or 70 thousand people there. It is absolutely sure these people did not see a body 64,000 miles in diameter over 100 times the diameter of the earth itself. All that one can say is that God caused to appear before their eyes the phenomenon they witnessed; and He did so miraculously in a way humanly inexplicable."

Here, therefore, is the story in brief of a great saucer sighting with thousands of witnesses.

Those who have dedicated every possible moment to the solution of this strangest of all mysteries can eventually find the unmatched pieces pulling together as if drawn by a magnet. It is not necessary to read the answers, for they stand like an array of soldiers awaiting orders. To the searcher no further questioning is necessary. At given intervals in history the gates to other planets have been opened up. Many elect of their own volition to come earthward so that they might help their beloved brothers whose status is one of lower evolution.

This is not part of our textbook training, therefore it is difficult for the masses to accept it. It is still more difficult to imagine greater evolvement than our own. At the same time, if we are intelligent we would know that life goes on in a continuous spiral. Evolution does not cease, not for one infinitesimal moment. It should not be unbelievable that when life is completed on one planet, it evolves to a higher vibration. It seems equally believable that we would of necessity be forced to accept some sort of preparation for the transition to the higher vibrations. This would be experienced in environment adaptation and would mean reciprocity on both sides. It stands to reason that it would be just as difficult for space beings to enter our environment without adaption as it would for us to enter their domain unprepared.

The coming of Diane has been accompanied by many of the same signatures that marked the appearance on earth of other Beatified Ones; those who have come down through religious history as Saints. The pathway of life is paved with the pebbles of skepticism, so one dare not become too enthusiastic when a great mystery is suddenly revealed. With ideals tarnished by cynicism, one cannot truly turn on the lights of the soul. It is still harder to stretch the elasticity of consciousness to embrace the supreme moments that come only occasionally through the years.

The article in question was a divine revelation to me, although it did not come as a surprise. If strange ships had been coming to Earth, perhaps since before our history began to be recorded, it is reasonable to assume that the facets of Divinity referred to as Saints did not necessarily come from a Heaven, but from some other planet.

We can only speculate on this point, but when the avenues of space are opened perhaps a few more of the pieces will fall into place and we will have the answers. Approximately one hundred years have passed since little Bernadette Soubrious, a peasant child, met the Lovely Lady of the Lourdes in a darkened grotto of France. Since that day millions from every part of the globe have made pilgrimages to the Shrine of the Holy Waters in search of health. There have been healings here quite as miraculous as the healings of Jesus.

Again, shortly after the turn of the century, three little shepherd children came to the fore with the Beautiful Lady of Fatima. At that time all of Europe congregated on the doorstep of Portugal. The Sun had come out of its orbit to greet the crowd. Another miracle had happened.

The story of Jeanne d' Arc needs no retelling here. The little mystic followed the voices of Heaven and won the Battle of Orleans.

A recital of miracles could go on and on for they are to be found in all sacred literature, etched on the tablets of time. Miracles are miracles until they have been eased down to a lower level of understanding. Now that the mysteries of the past have taken on new connotations, perhaps they will be given more consideration. This means that the time may have come for us to take our legends and stories of holy beings more literally. Before dismissing the thought lightly, wouldn't it be wiser to consider some of the corroborating factors? Perhaps many of our myths can now be cleared away by way of acceptance of extraterrestrials!

I am not trying to convince my readers that a flying saucer did appear over Fatima October. 13, 1917 nor can I say with certainty that the angelic beings, who have become a part of every child's religious education, come from the more advanced planets. But there is a uniformity in repetition that should not be completely ignored. There are too many parallels worthy of investigation.

Most of us have been conditioned to believe in some sort of heaven. The prophets know more about these heaven worlds than the average person. Whether wisely or not, we expect them to pave the way forward. Spectacle and miracles have heralded each facet of growth. As evolution has moved forward, the scattered fragments have assembled the abstractions and concretions and welded them together. We know that the abstractions of one era become the concretions of the next.

Diane made her first appearance to me in June,1939. I found her leaning against a gnarled old tree stump singing the song of Diane.

She came again in April, 1955. She was definitely not a spirit manifestation, but obviously created of a substance not of this earth. Since that time Diane has appeared on many occasions, not only to me, but to others. Today there is sufficient evidence to link her to the long line of mysteries. She came in the same miraculous manner as the Lady of Lourdes and the Lady of Fatima. She came as others have who have become revered in religious history. Diane bore the physical appearance of an earth being, yet she was clothed in the raiment of the angels. Culture and refinement stood out in every inch of her lithe and graceful body, a body as perfect as human form could be.

She was neither a myth nor a figment of the imagination, for her touch was physical. Her resonant voice was like chaste poetry.

Before the coming of strange ships to the skies I had pondered the thought many times: had Diane come from some heavenly realm; an etheric world somewhere out in space? If so, surely this was verification that we entertain visitors from other planets.

None of us know the answers, but we do know they are trying to open up the avenues of space. We are trying to wing our way to other planets. Space travel is no longer an alien concept, but rather has developed into a race among major powers to see who gets there first. We are no longer looking down, we are looking up. We have conquered lower space with our rapidly accelerated modes of travel. Now our sights are set on the moon and the planets.

To be sure, we are still figuring on an Earthly premise. We haven't yet learned that we must step out of the old frame of reference if we are going to entertain something that is beyond the scope of our understanding. If we are going to gain any measurable support we will be forced to tap the basic patterns. The Beautified Ones out of the past can furnish us with concrete examples.

The miracle of Fatima is similar in many ways to the appearance of Diane at a place where she was seen and heard by twenty-seven amazed persons. That same week four purported "mother ships" were seen over Palm Springs, California near my home. The sightings were reported by members of the Ground Observation Corps, and all skywatchers gave the same story. The mammoth craft were traveling at amazing speeds. They issued no tail fire and were completely noiseless. Following the usual behavior of Unidentified Flying Objects, they vanished into the nothingness before the eyes of the onlookers. The watchers all said the craft revealed a long row of odd looking portholes through which streamed a blue-white flame. Added to these accounts, a yellow or dangerous alert made newspaper headlines in Los Angeles.

There are still other facets to be considered. Bernadette Soubrious described the Heavenly Lady who appeared in the grotto of Lourdes as "being made of ivory and alabaster". She came attired in a white robe and as told by the little peasant girl: "sometimes it had a gleam of satin, yet it was like some unknown fabric, very delicate, ineffably snowy velvet . . . and again like a transparency."

The shepherd children of Fatima described their Lady "as made up of white radiance—whiteness more white than snow; or like snow that the sun shines through until it becomes crystalline." All came in times of stress, the gentle shepherds of humanity. Diane, like these others, came in a dazzling phosphorescent light.

Again I quote Diane from "Over The Threshold:"

"Many times I have been seen over the hallowed spots of the Earth. I have ministered to the sufferings on the bloody fields of battle. Child of Earth, I am the spirit of womanhood afloat on the sea of life. When changes are imminent it is the task of woman to usher in the new birth. I shall walk the streets of earth. I shall hover over your humanity until the day of transition comes. Some will see me in bodily form, others in my twin, shadowy body."

Who are these Blessed Ones, these patterns of Divinity ? Isn't it just possible that in days long past they were humans like ourselves? That through long centuries of living the good life, culturing the spiritual verities, they have at long last attained a stain of perfection? Is this the type of being we will find when we finally land our craft on the more advanced planets?

We know nothing about the hierarchies, the higher arcs of perfection. But if we once admit these deified ones into our consciousness, the questions mount up one after the other. Where did they come from? What is their mission on earth? It is fairly logical to assume that our higher learning must come from the higher arcs. In what other manner can higher teachings be transmitted to a lesser order? This same dimensional increase can be ours when we are willing to open the doors; when we can look beyond our mundane sphere of reference. We have built high fences around the Earth, but they evidently can go through the fences, instead of over them.

Today we are doing a turn about on this issue. Subjects dealing with paranormal phenomena, long in ill repute, are beginning to take on a new dignity. It is all a part of the breakthrough. In recent years, with such contemporary thinkers as Aldous Huxley, Gerald Heard, Aileen Garrett and Dr. J. B. Rhine all taking the lead, these long overlooked ideals have gone through a process of rejuvenation. However, the greatest strides have been made since the flying saucer era began.

What does it mean? Isn't it just possible they are coming to bring us knowledge and wisdom, to help us clean up our dirty Earth? It might be true that there has been some information withheld by national governments, but it is very possible they know less about this subject than those who have spent years in research. A four-star general may be an authority in his own field but is he capable of evaluating something he has never encompassed? Something that belongs to an alien world? He has been a part of earth life. His food and his shelter have come from the earth. His knowledge of space and what it contains does not go beyond his earthly yardstick.

The yardstick! We must create a new yardstick. But how and where are we going to begin? First we must dig out the old musty volumes of traditional literature. Rather than depending upon present day scientists, let us see what the prophets and the mystics have to say. They have had to change the yardstick many times. They have mastered many of the subtle sciences. It is said that the masters of old had secret powers we know nothing about. They had knowledge of that baffling law of materialization and dematerialization. If the alchemists of medieval times held these secrets, is it not possible for us to acquire them again? Is this the way to the answer to the great mystery? When we search in the pages of these musty volumes we find case histories too numerous to mention.

I recall an incident in Los Angeles several years ago. I had met, in a strange way, a kindly old gentleman who carried in his aura the wisdom of a sage. It was rumored he held the secret of materialization and dematerialization and I was determined to find out. He was hesitant at first. "So many scorn this old man," he said. But I persisted and soon I was witnessing one of the most amazing demonstrations of my life.

He took a fresh and perfect specimen of a white rose, dematerializing it before my eyes. In a few moments he brought it back, perfect in every petal. It remained in manifestation for a few moments and he repeated the performance. He then used a crushed, bruised flower in the experiment. He could dematerialize it as he had done in the first instance, but he was unable to bring it back again.

We have relegated this mysterious art to the ash heap because we have not understood it. We couldn't taste it, or experience some sort of sense reaction, so we were certain it did not exist.

This same strange phenomenon is related to the saucer mystery. When it is solved, the saucer question will doubtless also be solved. It is the task of the sensitive to bring the abstract patterns into concrete form. The sensitive is aware that the mechanism used is merely an extension of the physical senses, just as the space above the earth is an extension of the earth itself.

When the doorways to other planets have been opened, the world may change its viewpoint. Those who live each day within the shadow of absolute reality are convinced these messengers are coming now to bring forth the miracles. We should be waiting to greet them with the warmest of welcome. Quoting from "Over The Threshold:"

Diane has said; "There are plots of earth scattered over the face of the globe now being prepared as contact points between beings of earth and those from higher planets. These hallowed spots in the days to come will serve as holy shrines; clean spots where human regeneration will take place."

Little Bernadette and the shepherd children had their trials and their tribulations. Scorn and ridicule was heaped upon them. Those who dare to voice that which is outside the pale of the accepted norm must expect similar tribute. A great tribute goes to the Church for its acceptance of the fantastic as a realistic happening. Thousands of sick and wounded bodies have been healed as a result.

Today we took to our world leaders to pave the way for change. Perhaps we should look to the prophets and saints to break the chains of earthly woes. Does it really matter whether or not they come from an evanescent heaven-world or the more advanced planets? It is still a heaven-world to us.

UP RAINBOW HILL

CHAPTER NINE

What are these beings made of? If they come from planets more advanced than ours, could it be they are built of finer substances, more perfect materials? Human beings are bound to earth by the weight of gravity. Bone structures and flesh bodies provide us with earthly weight. As we adapt to higher frequencies, perhaps we will be able to drop the heavier substances and take on the more rarified essences. It needs no fantastic imagination to accept this theory as a working premise.

A recent internationally circulated newspaper story electrified the world, for it purportedly came from the brilliant mind of Carl Gustav Jung, world-renowned psychologist. It is said that Dr. Jung served as chief psychologist for the Aerial Phenomena Research Organization, UFO Filter Center, with headquarters at Alamagordo, New Mexico. In the news item he said:

"UFO phenomena are not mere rumor. A purely psychological explanation is ruled out by the fact that a large number of observations have proven inexplainable as natural phenomena."

He added that the credibility of the existence of UFO has been given by the fact that the United States and Canada have set up bureaus to compile reports on them.

But the most important statement of all coming from this eminent thinker is this: "The discs do not behave in accordance with physical laws, but as though they were without weight. They show evidence of intelligent guidance by quasi-human pilots for their accelerations are such that no normal human could survive."

Dr. Jung stated further: "Should the extra-terrestrial origin of the UFOs be proven, it might have the same effect on the human race that superior technology of western European had on primitive cultures. Just as the Pax Brittanica put an end to the disputes between the tribes of Africa, so our world could unroll its Iron Curtain and use it as scrap iron with all the millions of tons of guns, warships and munitions."

The voice of Dr. Jung was heard, but that voice was soon quieted. The repercussions from the article were thunderous; and a few days later this contemporary of Freud's retracted his statements, switching to a new tack and calling UFOs a result of "the world's psychological need of fantasy."

Strange as it seems, under pressure the world's greatest merchant in psychology denied his own theorizing on the very premise on which his world-accepted psychology stood. To quote the press:

"Doctor Carl Jung is convinced that people who think they have seen flying saucers just wanted to see them. Many people today are in need of fantasy."

"The 83-year-old psychologist finally came to the conclusion that people who claim to have seen flying saucers are searching for a new savior, and are reviving the ancient savior myths to satisfy their psychological needs.

"'Their minds are cornered by the bad situation in which our world is today,' he said. "They are in need of answers to their anxious questions, which nobody can give them. That is why they let their fantasy run on the lines of flying saucers and similar objects."

In the light of two diametrically opposite opinions evolving from the same brain, it makes one wonder what sort of pressure might have been brought to bear to cause this man to retract his original story? Was it ridicule alone? For one who had become accustomed to fame, perhaps ridicule bruised his ego. The scathing remarks of reporters were not easy to take. A paper in Vancouver, British Columbia, stated it this way : "The silly season has come late this year, what with Arabs, summits and royal visits. But the inevitable can be delayed only so long, and now, sure enough, the flying saucers are back. I can only say for certain that these things are not mere rumor, something has been seen, and that 'they show signs of intelligent guidance by quasi-human pilots,' says Carl Jung. What more evocative adjective could there be than 'quasi-human'? What more suggestive of little green men from Mars ?"

For those who have delved deeply into the subject, it would seem that each facet of Jung's brilliant concepts carry the weight of authenticity. On the occasions when Diane has appeared she has in every way resembled an Earthly being. She walked and talked. She carried on profound discourses, then with the tips of her tiny fingers on my shoulder she would vanish into nothingness.

Thousands have watched the saucers disappear in the same mysterious manner. If we accept the premise that they are functioning a full octave higher than the frequencies of our planet Earth, it is reasonable to assume they would not carry around weight bodies. On the lower arcs we live in a world of gravity.

On the higher arcs they would live in a world of levity. This being so, their bodies could be almost identical to ours in outward appearance, yet at the same time they would be completely weightless.

I quote from the final chapter in "Over The Threshold":

"The days of miracles are here now. It is time for the great mystery to be revealed. The answer is to be found in the matrix of the cosmos. When we conquer pure abstraction, we will have reached the goal. Gravity has been the enigma of the ages. From birth to death we have been bound to Earth levels by the bonds and fetters of gravity. Gravity has forced us to remain within the boundaries of Earth.'"

UP RAINBOW HILL

As my books will prove, I have held to the Jungian theory from the beginning. To make this a little more explicit for those unfamiliar with it, I mean that when primordial or creative substance is stepped down in density, to an Earthly level, it must have flesh and blood and bone in its makeup. Jung's statement that they appear to be quasi-beings is genuinely reasonable to accept.

Diane has said:

"The physical body has its birth in physical substance. It grows slowly over the years to the age of maturity, then gradually it deteriorates and disintegrates. The true spiritual body is both transmutable and translatable because it has been broken down into finer particles until it becomes creative essence."

Every living being is bound to the wheel of life but that wheel revolves on many levels. We are all links in the long red line of Infinity. Far back in our nebulous memory is a record of wild, uncultivated wastes; mountains that have sunk beneath the ocean waves, flat lands that have been raised up to become the highest mountains. We have strayed from the mainline many times, yet the sturdy link has never been broken. Somewhere buried in our hearts and souls we can still feel the pulse of the Father Mother God.

All things, physical and natural, have had to learn to adapt to environment. We might ask why it is that Earth lines must carry around solid, heavy bodies when subtle ones would be much handier. It is because we live on an earthy Earth. Our seeds are planted in its subsoil. This is simply told in the legends of the American Indians. The older Indians believed that man was fashioned from the Earth's clay; that the white clay made the white people, the yellow clay made the yellow people, the red clay made the red people. Well, why not ? In the chain of evolutionary events, all things are possible. We're startled, are we not, when we look back at the changes that have transpired in one short generation. We cannot stretch the imagination far enough to look back and see what happened thousands of years ago. There is a definite tie between each dimension, between all realms of life. We have obscured those dimensions because our roads are cluttered with misunderstandings and the injustices heaped upon our fellow beings. When the roadways are cleared of human debris, then we will see clearly into the past and the future.

It is the task of the few endowed with extrasensory vision to do this. Stepped up vision permits one to penetrate the veil. Vision helps to coerce the spirit into giving up its treasures in the form of concepts, which later emerge into actual reality. Divine knowing without divine realization falls fallow on unproductive soil. Vision without realization is pure delusion. It leads nowhere. It was the illustrious Spanish philosopher lbn Gabirol who said: "The greater the degree to which vision penetrates color and pierces shape and quantity and substance, the more obscure being becomes to it." Real vision leads to transcendence. It provides invisible wings with which to soar into space. In the past decade many have had their mental faculties awakened. Others have touched the fringe of true science. Some have been privileged to join forces with the exalted ones. Literally thousands have emerged from the dense fog of materialism to realize at last that there are superior forces and founts of power from which men can draw new strength, new faith, new knowledge.

Hermes Trismegetis said centuries ago: "As above, so below." This means, does it not, that we all have the same potential powers within us. We are no longer swimming in fantasy and illusion, but the abstractions we have embraced have been transmuted into realities. Many have learned to ride waves of spiritual rhythm. A few have been carried far out into the sea of space. Some have touched the higher arcs where they have met the hierarchies. When we can view these higher arcs for ourselves we will understand what is meant by finer, more rarified grades of substance.

Was this what Doctor Jung meant when he referred to the spaceship pilots as "quasi-human?" The human structure is built for Earth living. It functions in the body of the Earth. It is wrapped up in the soil of the Earth. Human beings confined to a crystalized earthly existence seldom soar very far from their single dimension. They know nothing of the beyond because it has not come within the category of sense reaction.

Yet, the Bible tells us we have a spiritual body as well as a natural body. A body within a body, with one composed of finer energies. When one learns to control these finer energies, he has command over life itself. He can bring it forth at will. Those who have dedicated their lives to the greater cause have proven beyond doubt that these energies exist. Yogis and holy men have performed feats comparable to those of the Christ. This being true, it is easier to comprehend the idea that perhaps extraterrestrials live in a world composed of these finer essences; that their physical bodies are made up of like substances. We might also dare to presume that in our new life cycle, we, too, will function in these highly energized bodies. The "new" requires specialized attention; one pointedness that can burn through to realization. Knowledge is not gained by skirting the fringe, but going through to the heart of knowledge.

The world today is slim conscious. Men and women alike are trying to rid themselves of their paunches, jowls and double-chins. Methods for contouring the body and keeping fit form a big part of today's national advertising campaigns. Is this an accident or is it a coincidence? Every thinker knows that the body is only a shell. It is just as difficult to wrench ourselves free from this hulk we call our body as it is to wrench ourselves free from the worn out form we call our globe. Just as we are trying to regenerate fat laden cells, we are trying to regenerate this gas bag we call "Earth."

The idea of abandonment—even for something better—fills us with panic. We enjoy the familiar and life on a new octave is something we have not yet experienced. Those who are preparing themselves live in fanciful hopes that a miracle will happen and one day they will soar away on a new Noah's Ark. They will exult to the heavens to be free at last from a world seething with poisonous plasmas.

As man is, so is the planet on which he resides. Each planet has its own life structure. Perhaps they also have cellular bodies, their molecular bodies, and their electronic bodies.

Physical bodies are the slow motioned. They crawl, they walk, they run. But it is impossible to project a physical body into space without it falling of its own weight. When gravity is conquered, either by a miracle of science or the slow evolutionary march, then perhaps we will be able to rise to the higher octaves. The ultimate is an extremity far beyond our conception. In our present stage of evolution we cannot go beyond the bounds of our solar system. We cannot think beyond that point. Why? Because it is the terminus of our boundary sense; a pattern cycle formed eons ago.

Wittingly or unwittingly, we are making some daily contribution toward a new pattern. Those who understand lend their consciousness by believing in it. They know deep within that one day it will come to pass.

The Earth has changed its form many times. The customs and habits of men have changed, too. The bones of each passing age are to be found in the stratified remains of the Earth. As time passes, many treasures hidden from the gaze of humans will be revealed, for each advancing cycle must preserve the seeds of the cycle that is closing.

The restlessness of humanity is a good indication of the change. Mental hospitals are overflowing with the remnants of a hapless group of worriers. Every hot mineral spa is working overtime trying to re-energize soul-deadened bodies. Arthritis and other crippling ailments are on the increase. Heart disease ranks as the nation's leading health problem. Not one unit of humanity can escape, yet few realize what it is they are trying to escape. We are clinging to our woes as rust clings to a worn out chain.

The Space Age is upon us. We cannot linger at the crossroads trying to decide which way to go. We must rise or we must fall. Those who have dedicated their lives to the task of helping in this transition period can see the walls of Earth crumbling like the walls of Jericho.

How can we swim out of these stagnant pools of slime and pollution?

First, our vision must be directed to the higher realms. As our thoughts soar upward we will find new levity in our bodies. The weight will fall away like fog before the Sun. We will no longer crave heavy, indigestible foods. We will reject the body stuff that adds weight to the physical structure. We will feel a rarified freshness such as we have not experienced before. Bodies teleportively drifting off into space will be commonplace. When the body is-rid of its heavy, ponderous substance, projection will be the heritage of all.

Impossible?

UP RAINBOW HILL

Not at all. Jesus Christ made Himself weightless, H{e walked upon the waters. He fed the multitudes on loaves and fishes, created from pure essence. He came back after His translation to greet His disciples. It is said He ate with them; He drank with them. While His physical body had been destroyed, His molecular body was still intact.

These accounts have been set down in Biblical records as miracles. The true meaning and significance has remained obscured in our Earthly concepts. With this new knowledge will come wisdom; the wisdom to do all things.

Nature creates no accidents. Inspiration is the offspring of spirit. Doctor Carl Jung transformed myth into realism with his monumental theories of psychology. Meandering in the realms of the fantastic, he found a way to release twisted, gnarled minds so they could function clearly.

It is apparent that his own thinking apparatus was working well when he said that "...flying saucers seemed to be guided by superior quasi-human beings." Nor was he far wrong when he said that humanity is seeking a Savior.

If we're intelligent, we know that we cannot save ourselves. In every crisis there have been messengers from higher climes to lead the way.

Doctor Jung says in his retraction: "Today many people are out in search of fantasy." Jungian psychology is based on fantasy. He is the greatest merchant of fantasy of our times.

Fantasy and fact fit together like black-and-white and like all related opposites. Is it fantasy when thousands of new human channels have been opened up? When lives have been changed overnight? Is it fantasy that we can now talk about space travel with some assurance of certainty? Is it fantasy to have fireside chats about free energy just as we did about radio and television a few years ago? There are those who feel certain that we will soon be fueling our operations with the natural energies of the universe. Perhaps Doctor Jung is right. Perhaps we are in need of this kind of fantasy.

The UFO era has released us into a new dimension in thinking. We are no longer groping in that new world. It is beginning to make plenty of sense.

UP RAINBOW HILL

As the life force is stepped down from its original God created founts, it naturally gains density and weight. Matter exists in varying stages of density whether we can see it or not. The gross substance does not stop at the Earth plane, but goes down, down, down to the hell-pits below. That which is dense grows more dense until the time comes for it to change. This is happening today. We are rising although we are not yet aware of the ascent. Many of our teenagers know it; youngsters scarcely out of their swaddling clothes are talking glibly about free energy. The space age is no enigma to them. That which is beyond the understanding of the average adult, many of these teenagers inherited at birth. They will unlock the doors of space if we do not. That which we have dreamed of they will find.

In the days ahead the most ruthless government will have a difficult time convincing youth that war is virtuous. The new crop coming up will find the magical fields. They will not find the fields while they are fighting to conquer the Earth, but while they are reconnoitering the unknown. They will tackle the job of penetrating space as their forebearers tilled the soil. The things we have looked to as our supply sources will be doomed. Airborne things will take their place. Many new and hidden talents will be brought to the surface. Humanity will experience a different order of life when men live together in peace and harmony. Trial and error methods will be obsolete and tabooed.

We will find the answers in the arcane scrolls. We will learn to mold our lives from the essence, just as the baker kneads his dough.

CHAPTER TEN

While spectacular display ushered in the UFO era, it would at first seem that the days of space phenomena have passed. Did the spectacle help us to better understand the new concepts? Had it not been for the drama attached to it, the "sighting fever" would have worn itself out long ago. That which originally seemed fantastic is commonplace today.

Perhaps the best proof of outer space phenomena was the coming of the lovely Diane. She has been seen in many places by diverse individuals, but on October 3, 1957, she appeared in a public lecture hall, the Woman's Club of Fontana, California, by way of transfiguration. It was a public meeting, the audience made up of believers and unbelievers alike. About half way through the lecture I felt my body growing very warm. It had nothing to do with the hall temperature, for it was cool out of doors. At the end of the meeting, a number from the audience rushed to me, breathless from what they had witnessed. It seemed Diane had stood on the platform where I had stood in all her unsurpassed loveliness. Through some strange electronic force the cellular atoms of my body were dissolved, and the fine essence body of Diane took over. I present excerpts from letters received from some of the witnesses.

Mrs. Eleanor of Fontana writes:

"I saw transposed over Dana Howard's body, the figure of a beautiful woman, very young, with long golden hair, a very slim body and small waistline. She seemed to glow in golden light, and her gown flowed gently in flowing layers of gossamer like substance. . . ."

Mrs. Trudy Allen of Fontana relates it this way:

"On the night of October 3, 1957, I sponsored Dana Howard in a lecture at the Woman's Clubhouse, Fontana. During the lecture my attention was drawn to her appearance. All of a sudden I became aware of a very youthful, charming vibrant being, just sparkling with beauty; the kind words cannot begin to convey. I said to myself : 'She is positively beautiful; in fact she actually looks like Dana's description of Diane. This lasted about fifteen minutes. I cannot recall anything she said for I was so overcome with the transcendent beauty that was shining forth."

Jean Ban of Ontario, California, says:

"It was a portrayal of dazzling light, color and beauty such as I have never before experienced."

Shirley Regis, of Fontana asked this question:

"Does Diane ever appear in you? I couldn't believe it et first. It seemed like an illusion, so I closed my eyes tight. She was absolutely gorgeous. Too fantastic for words to describe."

While the majority of this audience were allowed to see this lovely being, a few present seemingly were not so fortunate. They were aware, it seems, that something unusual was happening, but they did not know what it was. Perhaps that something within themselves had not yet been awakened. It is possible that we, too, must be "lifted" from our cellular bodies before we can see with the vision of transcendence. However, the future may prove that this is the source of all true science.

What does a peculiarly strange body heat have to do with transcendence? It seems that such a heat state frequently accompanies unusual phenomena. Heat seems to create a fusion so that the cellular body can be released and the molecular can take over. Many unorthodox healers are familiar with this principle: the catalytic influence of one body over another. In this way the primordial essence, or dynamically charged plasma, is abstracted from one body (a twin form) and created in the ether. In this situation the physical body serves as an anchorage, the weight necessary to hold the mass of substance to the concrete Earth.

When these new, scientifically correct ideas are made known generally, then we will be on the eve of many miraculous happening.

What is the center of gravity? Where can it be found? It is at the hub of all density, at the center of every living cell, but it is often obscured. When this heavy obstruction is dissolved, or transmuted, the force is permitted to come through in all its electrical luminosity.

Mineral matter represents the extreme of density on our planet. The more mineralized a man is, the more inert he is. And since habits are formed in chemical substance, a man who becomes set in his habits simply stagnates.

Inner changes may take place in "the twinkling of an eye." But outer change is imperceptibly slow. The interferences we face daily are the concentrates of density; pollution that has gathered and that hangs over an area like a bank of smog. If these densities are not removed constantly the age-laden cells develop into age laden tissues. The body loses its elasticity and tone. Habits, good or bad, eventually become firm and fixed as cement blocks. Concentration is the shell of reality. When the shell becomes too rigid a new wave of violence blasts it away. A new war begins.

The greatest hope in our world of despair is faith. We all look hopefully toward a peaceful world. Every sane human being is sickened by the thought of war. He is weary of an economy based on war. We would all like to dwell in a land of milk and honey, secure in the knowledge that a ray of justice still flows through the stream of life. To rise above man-made systems and man-made beliefs is our hopeful prayer.

The source of true peace is not to be found in a ritual of magic, but in spiritual security. We glibly prate that the universe belongs to God, yet we will fight to the last man to take it away from Him. Earthman cannot conceive a system beyond mine and thine. Few on earth have truly grasped the principle that there is but ONE, that all things come from HIM.

Earthman lives fast and furiously through his short life span, and then passes on to he knows not what. The insignia of death is his breastplate of armor. He has placed the stamp of death on every living thing. Dedicated to chaos, chaos is his life's pattern. He expects war. He prepares for war. He lives or he dies in the war he has created. He knows that one day his universe will fall; that the cycle will come to an end. "But, it won't happen in my lifetime," he rationalizes, "so why should I care?"

It was the homespun philosopher Will Rogers who said : "When you live life to its fullest there is nothing on Earth to be frightened of. It is a privilege to pass on." If we could have some absolute certainty of survival, how different it would be! If we knew we had nothing to fear of death we would then be able to live life to the fullest.

To know ONENESS is to know peace. It is to know peace that is permanent with none of the roar of battle behind it. Peace cannot come until we have purged ourselves of greed land selfishness. When man separated himself from his source, he separated himself from paradise. When he began to use science viciously he lost touch with the Source of his science. United States Army General Omar N. Bradley has said, "...we have many men of science, but too few men of God. We have grasped the mystery of the atom, and rejected the Sermon on the Mount."

Man is made in the "image and likeness of God." Creation springs from the godhead. Man in his true essence is God incarnate. He came from God and one day he will find his way back to Source. But in the long trek through the winding cycles he has met many pitfalls. He was tumbled into the deep, dark holes. He absorbs the lowered vibrations which blind him and make him stumble from his path. The farther away he slips the more pollution he gathers. Eventually in the mass of slime he accumulates he can no longer navigate. If he could view this vile stuff he would see it as a dark, murky mass, tinged with hateful greens, ugly reds, colors off on a binge. Millions of hunan auras are filled and running over with this vile corruption. The hapless victim is forced to breathe the stuff into his lungs and his blood stream.

All things begin from the invisible. Those whose vision has been awakened can clearly see our Earth as made up of fine strands somewhat like silken threads. We call them "the threads of life." Through these threads flows a milky substance—the essence. When played upon by electrical fire, creation begins. Every living thing is created in the self-same way. As the first essence is stepped down from its original Source it gathers the substance of the lowered vibrations. The residue released from our distorted thoughts is like sediment in the bottom of a bottle. In time it crystallizes into a solid. This must be blasted away or dissolved. The blasting creates more of the same grade of stuff to be reassembled again. Transmutation gets rid of it forever. If we had attenuated vision we would see our atmosphere filled with this flotsam. It would seem like fog banks of putrification. This is the decay absorbed into our bodies in the food we eat, in the water we drink.

We cannot be truly healthy until our thoughts are purified. Our world will be healthy when we put health into our world. With intensified vision we would see these areas of crystallization. They would be as black as stygian night. We would see the now and then Satanic fires in the distance. These fires are fueled by the germs of war. They have been burning since time immemorial and will continue to burn so long as we fuel them with hate.

Those who possess extrasensory vision tell us that these areas are filled with grotesque, ugly creatures, entities that live to enjoy their suffering. War on earth deepens their suffering and since their existence is inextricably entwined with ours, our suffering increases in proportion. It is hard for us to accept these outcasts as part of the universe we live in, but only because they have not been considered in our conditioning. They belong to the Source as we do. Like the prodigal son, they have strayed far from home. But one day they, too, will come back. Although they have broken the threads through which the milk and honey flows, eventually the threads will be caught up and repaired.

We can help with that task, too. How? When we know that each infinitesimal part of His vast creation is in a constant state of change; when we realize that every grain of sand ultimately must become a unit of spiritual force, then we shall know that even these hateful forms will one day become pleasing to look upon. Each living thing must eventually move forward. As it traverses time's vastness, it gains in insight and knowledge. It finally must rise in the scheme of evolution. Man leaves the House of God connected to the strings of creation. When he severs these threads he starts falling toward the lower grottoes.

When he arrives, the threads no longer glisten with a golden aura, but are black and rotten. The disconsolate beings on this elemental level would have just as difficult a time reaching the Earth plane as we have reaching the throne of God.

It is from these hateful grottoes that the pattern of war is cast. Steeped in violence, these creatures live for violence. They live to devour; to consume. They live in a crucified consciousness; a state of bondage. In a mad trance they seek freedom, but they have no idea where to find it.

War pulls us down to these little hells. War brings us ever closer to the source of evil. Once down in the muck, our souls are scarred, our eyes blinded to good. As we put out one fire another is lighted. This has gone on through the centuries. It will go on and on until the pattern of war has been completely destroyed.

Today as never before the masses are sick of war. They want nothing to do with any venture that smacks of war, even though it might mean their daily bread. If it were put to a vote, the great majority of people would prefer to take a chance and give up their luxuries rather than face the inevitability of a nuclear conflict. Few are ready or willing to endure another horrific war.

This attitude is another step toward the final breakthrough. But will it do any good? We know we cannot stockpile nuclear bombs around the globe without someone igniting the torch. We cannot continue to prepare for war and at the same time cry out for peace They are not of the same breed. War is part of the spectacle; the band-playing, flag-waving, of human feet stomping in a parade of violence masquerading as a means to peace.

We are moving off into space. At no time in our long cyclic history have we been so ripe for change. It is easier to change the pattern today than at any time we have known. When an alcoholic can embrace a concept larger than himself he can be cured. This same principle applies to war drunks. The challenge of outer space is far more gripping than the battle hymn.

The abolishment of war is not a task isolated persons or groups can accomplish. It means pulling together on the same stout rope. It means unity and like-mindedness. Nature pyramids by elevating all!

There will be the die-hards. Until the gas bag collapses they will not know that it has been punctured.

But peace will not be postponed. It will come in one way or another. We are at the end of a cycle and there can be no more special fruit for the few. We can elevate ourselves only by elevating all.

Doctor Jung is right—we are seeking a Savior. We are trying once more to revive the old "savior myths." We need those from on high to lead us toward the hill from where we can see the light. The "savior," however, might not be an avatar this time, but an advanced being from across the seas of space.

When will all of this take place ? This question furrows many brows. But the answer is relatively simple. It is entirely up to us. How quickly can we change our viewpoint? When are we going to throw away the old yard-stick? We cannot fight our way through space.

How can we redirect the momentum? How can we blaze the new trail? The pioneers of the early days of our country's growth braved every hard-ship to make life more worth while for their families. Death stalked every inch of their path but the adventurers, imbued with the spirit of adventure, kept on. There were hoped for rewards at the end of the trail.

Diane has said: "Earthlings must be baited with reward."

Again she has said: "Many have asked what is to be gained by open-ing up the avenues of space. To land craft on other planets. My daughter, when the spaceways have been opened up a tidal wave of good things will flow in. Many Earthlings will be endowed with strange new talents. In some the prophetic insight will be awakened. Thousands upon thousands will have the burdens of life lifted. Others will be healed of bodily ills, and so on."

Perhaps there will be rewards greater than anything we have ever known on Earth. Those who have caught a fleeting glimpse of golden empires (if only on their mystical excursions) have said they would be willing to forfeit the best on earth for the least in other planetary gifts. Warring nations would be willing to forget their wars, their blood-letting, if they were sure the harvests were great enough. For those who have been wrapped in selfishness, it is hard to realize that there might be superior forces in the universe, that far out in the unknown even greater spoils are waiting.

But when we finally realize that there is a magic mountain from which all things spring and that within that fountain we will find peace, then life will be worth living. The Space Age can bring us true brotherhood, the Alpha and Omega fulfilled. It can bring us that sovereign orderliness that anchors the known to the unknown. It is as immutable as the stars themselves. When we find that law of balance where center meets center, we will be on our way to the goal.

CHAPTER ELEVEN

Jesus said, "The last enemy to overcome is death."

It is hoped that the opening of the avenues of space will help us to overcome the fear of death. During the last decade there has been a broadening of knowledge. Extended education has partially implanted the idea of survival in our minds. Many believe the time is close when we will be able to pierce the veil scientifically and see for ourselves that there is no death. We will then know that it is not the length of life that counts, but how one lives it. Death will no longer be looked upon as a thief in the night that leaves a gap in the lives of loved ones.

The solution to all things is to be found in the "just-beyondness." We first have to learn how to adjust to the shifting scenes.

While we have moved ahead slowly on this ponderous Earth, nothing remains wholly static. At the peak of each spiral we find something new to be added. Transcendence over time and space means the coming of miracles. Perhaps it will mean a great change in human status, too. Jesus, in raising Lazarus from the dead, proved to us that we can change from a piece of decaying flesh to a healthy individual in a moment of time. We have believed ourselves superior to all living things, but we have proof all around us that we are still in an elemental stage of existence. We have sung lullabys to our children. We have lulled ourselves to sleep with the same sing-song.

UP RAINBOW HILL

Now the time has come to grow up.

The wail and cry everywhere is "Where am I going to find security?" We will find security when we accept survival. When we are certain there is no death. The fear behind all fears is the coming of the reaper. When there is no more fear of becoming "unglued", when we know that the cohesive fluid that holds us together can be replaced, that life goes on after the cumbersome body has passed to dust, then we will be genuinely rid of our fears,

The evidence of our degenerating structure is to be seen on all sides. Unless we are steeped in morbidity we're not entertained. Unless there is a murder on every page of a book, a death scene in every radio and TV skit, we think we have been cheated. Morbidity holds a vital place in man's consciousness. It means more to him than the hope of some beautiful future.

Morbidity is an ally of death. Destruction is a powerful magnet and we are being drawn to it like moths to a street light. Each current brings another wave toward the grave. When we take our vicarious joys in the woes of others we attract woe to ourselves. Each new horror sets up a war between the devils within and the devils without. When one passes from life, taking with him his bag of decayed "thought stuff," he takes his troubles with him to the other side of the veil. When one can "translate" into the next dimension, he finds a flood-tide of blessings awaiting him. If one has worked toward a life's fulfillment, death is just another step forward; a procession into the larger cycle of life. This is immortality; living in eternal peace.

Every experience comes to an end. When a task is completed death is a gentle release to the next rung of the ladder.

I recently witnessed an outstanding example of natural death. The angels came for one of my good friends, Emza Hazlewood of Palm Springs, California. Emza had been a devout follower of the interstellar beliefs since the day Kenneth Arnold told the world his story. She bought the first copy of "Over The Threshold." It had not dawned upon her family and close friends that she was a sick woman. Her ambitions were still at white heat. She gave freely to others. She worked at her profession every day. But finally the ravages of cancer were made evident. Her body wracked with pain, the doctors gave her little time to live. Emza believed in miracle healing. She could have resorted to this method, but deep within she knew her task on Earth was finished. She longed to take up life on one of the more advanced planets. She was sure that death would release her to this new land of promise.

With the light of spiritual zeal in her eye, she called two of her daughters to her bedside. They believed in the things their mother believed in. When she told them she was going on a journey into an unknown land, they were not sad or emotionally unstrung. When she told them the new world beckoned, that her suitcase was packed for flight, her fine daughters understood.

Their mother had always been a Stoic. She had taught them to look upon this change as a great adventure. Together they discussed the beauties she would find beyond the veil. Day by day they began to look forward to the experience with a quiet enthusiasm. As the time closed in, their Stoicism grew. It was wonderful to know that there was no terror to strike down its victim; no fear of the unfamiliar. Mother and daughters were ready. The young women were sure their mother was going to change her worn out Earthly garment for a new robe of whiteness. They knew she was not going to the land of the dead, but rather transiting from a world of time to a world of space. Henceforth she would become a pupil in the school of a new life. There would be no pushing or racing toward an uncertain tomorrow. There would be no sorrowing nostalgia. No more carrying about the weight of the world on her frail shoulders.

Nor would there be word-laden books to ponder. In the pause in the new eternity there would be illuminating discourses by unseen mentors. It was like awaiting the day of some gala event. The days passed, but they were so packed with glorious anticipation that even the convulsions of pain were bearable. Emza wore a smile on her face, an illuminated light in her eye.

Suddenly she thought of the garment of earth she was wearing. It did not belong to her, really. It had merely been loaned for the duration of one short life span. Science was seeking an answer to the cancer scourge. Perhaps her cast-off garment might furnish a clue. Nearing the end she told her daughters of her decision. Her body was to be donated to Loma Linda Medical School. This was her final gesture to the Earth she was leaving behind.

With her last breath she told them of the beauties she would meet, of the youthful body that would soon be hers. Emza Hazlewood passed from the mortal frame happy in the belief that life is eternal.

The time will come when the fear of death will be no more. This terror that struck deep into the heart of man back in the days of his primitive beginning helped him to grow. War and its conquering formed the premise upon which he lived. He entered the plane of death with fear and trembling. He expected to meet Satan, and Satan was there to meet him. The terrors his mind harbored were amplified many times. The sufferings he anticipated he received in full measure.

Human beings have been conditioned to fear the end. But a few go to their Maker without pangs of apprehension of the unknown. Although the last drop of sap has been sucked from their bodies, they cling to the fleshly form with a tenacious grip.

Today scientists are seeking the answer to the riddle of after-life. There are those in every age who dedicate their efforts to finding the solution to this puzzle. One-hundred years ago two frail young women living in Rochester, New York, opened the door an inch or two. The Fox Sisters and their rappings have brought consolation to thousands as they neared the end. While they are derided to this day, the consciousness generated by both believers and charlatans alike, has paid rich dividends. Even those steeped in sin want to have some assurance that they do live on.

It is a wonderful feeling to believe; to be able to go out of life filled with the anticipation of meeting loved ones who have gone before. When all doubts have been cleared away and we realize that the human body is merely a temporary house of clay, the soul can speed on its endless journey back to the Fountain of Source.

And now the inevitable question. Why must we go around and around on this treadmill called life? Why physical existence at all? Why an Earth? Why a solar system? Why a universe? The answers elude us all. We do not know. The sages of wisdom tell us that to be complete a soul must know all experiences. Each planet furnishes some of that needed knowledge. Each life is a guide post to the greater life. As man learns to live with himself, he must also learn to live with others. Each encounter with life furnishes something necessary to the soul-something that has not been fulfilled. This is life. It is the way of life.

As it is with man, so it is with nations, planets, the universe—all Life. At one time we internalize. At another we externalize. Man on the Earth plane lives for Earthly glory. He lives to enjoy the pleasures of Earth. He has lived to conquer through power. But in all his searching he has not found happiness.

In reaching toward space we are seeking the resurrected life. Before we can attain to that realm of resurrection we must rid ourselves of our crucified consciousness. "For since by man came death , by man came also the resurrection of the dead. For as in Adam all die . . even so in Christ, shall all be made alive." I Corinthians 15:21-22.

This means, does it not, that there is no death. It is plainly written that death means transition. We live for a time, in a mortal house of clay but when the short interlude is over we move on to a larger, more expansive home. This is the seed that must be planted in humanity's garden.

UP RAINBOW HILL

CHAPTER TWELVE

Many have asked: "Does the breakthrough mean that our days of plodding and poverty will be over? Will humanity abandon its economic struggle when it finds the release it has prayed for through the ages?"

If we can trust to the future and are willing to become an integral part of that future there is every reason to believe a balanced economy will come, too. We cannot cling to the old and expect the new to manifest. As Abraham Lincoln once said: "'We cannot be half slaves and half free." Unless we can forget our traditions we will go around on the same treadmill until something drastic comes along to wipe the slate clean.

The coming of strange spacecraft has made the world do a little thinking on its own. It has given many a new resurgence in faith. But are we big enough to take advantage of it? Will we possess the courage to reach out to pluck the fruits from the New Tree of Life? First we must convince ourselves that the change has already taken place in the subconscious realm. The old habit-mold must be destroyed before the new can operate. With disaster threatening on all sides, it will take time for alien ideas to unfold as realities. We have been slowly creeping toward this threshold of paradise and now that we are close to transition most of us are too soul-deadened with the struggle to open our eyes to look upon it.

How can we be made aware of the change ? Many must learn through absorption, by getting acquainted and associating with like-minded individuals. Thousands have been afraid to voice their innermost feelings. They did not want to be pelted with ridicule. Where there is a great yearning in the soul to know the way will be opened up. Once humanity can become a part of something bigger; when the boundaries of the thought-world begin to widen and the doors of the mind are opened, new knowledge will flow in like the clear, sparkling waters of a running stream.

Desire forges the greatest chain on earth. UFOs started the mad race. Flying saucers speeded up the urge to explore the unknown. Their speed and maneuverability baffled even the most hardheaded skeptics. They may not have been new objects, but they introduced a new force.

Today there are two camps of saucer enthusiasts: those who believe the answer will be found in sightings alone and those who believe in "contacteeism." Those in the first group scorn the government for withholding information. They sneer at those who have claimed contact.

What is contacteeism ? Who are the chosen? Had it not been for the contacts, flying saucers would have been forgotten long ago. The hope of meeting these extraterrestrials in the flesh, not sightings, has kept the idea alive. When interest wanes, intensity wanes. We are building consciousness to help us enter the Space Age. Technology must be advanced beyond our Earthly advancement before we can find our way through. Science must build a new road.

We recognize the chosen by their works. But, as always, "many are called but few are chosen." We've had only a foreshadowing of things to come. It needs no special degree of seer-ship today to predict the coming of future events, for each and every one of us is a potential prophet. Prophetic vision and the infusion of wisdom is no longer the sole right of the long haired, psalm-singing Earth-gods. The founts of knowledge are open to all.

Within the saucer groups, the word channeling has become commonplace. This process is carried on in the privacy of dimly lit homes, just as seances were once the vogue. I have met channelers from every walk of life; electronic engineers, ministers, teachers and, at the same time, the gas-station attendant and the boy who delivers the evening paper. They are all there, hoping for a signal, a sign, a strange word.

What is channeling? It is using the human mind as a focal point of contact. Making direct touch with the founts of knowledge. The materialist would call it concentration, the religionist meditation, but it is through the alembic of the human mind that the visible connects the invisible. It is the "bow" of the rainbow. It is the one way to touch the source of creation.

Life is for the purpose of growth. Without growth we stagnate and die. We have grown to become the greatest nation of the age. It was a major advance from feudalism to capitalism, a step downward from feudalism to communism. In the middle path we find no "ists" or"'isms" but a true, workable principle; a cooperative system, not a competitive one.

Specialization precedes universalization. In universalization we find the equation we are seeking. The glories we create in fantasy one day are the realities we enjoy in fact the next. Fact is but a point in crystallization. It is as impermanent as the gusty wind.

We cannot hold back the rainbow any more than we can hold back the dawn. It shows in the heavens after a storm. One does not need a university sheepskin to know that our money system is worn out. The same formula has been mixed up in the feed grinder for centuries. It served its purpose at the time it was conceived, but it has been totally outmoded.

When our forebears landed on these shores they were met by a strange race of beings, the Red Indians. Today we own their lands, bought with a few gaudy trinkets. Some will expect to do the same thing when we land our craft on other planets. We have lived our lives in a material world, measuring our values in terms of possessions. We have watched those possessions come into existence and pass away. With great reluctance we have come to accept the dictum that you can't take it with you. In the early days of our planet we tried to do that, too. The opening of ancient tombs has revealed wheat, corn and costly jewels, to say nothing of millions in gold. These things were still there, undisturbed. They were not taken across the borderline of death.

UP RAINBOW HILL

It is right and fitting that new channels must be created if we are going to bring to fruition the greatness that lies hidden in the folds of space. When the human mind is fully opened to the new concepts of other planets, they will no longer be millions of miles away, but practically on our doorstep. While this is vaguely acceptable to some, the thought of "contacteeism" is not. Perhaps this is so because they have not been contacted themselves. If anyone dares to claim communication with a space being he is called a liar without a hearing.

Whether he is willing to believe it or not, the contactee is the subjective link with objective reality. The subjective is the feminine or creative side. Without the polarities there would be no existence. Many are contactees, without being aware of it. But without the contactee we would still be wholly in the dark. Those who are open minded in their investigations have found themselves steaming ahead. As they embrace one new concept another presents itself. Out of this group will come the great leaders of tomorrow. They will have no old ideas to discard. They will have grown up with the new ideas. They will no longer theorize for they will have reached the mountaintops themselves; from there they can view the whole wide universe. At the pinnacle they will be able to balance values, the objective against the subjective, the material against the spiritual. With a complete change in viewpoint of the masses, the rest will happen quickly. They will be fascinated at the changes taking place within themselves. And then they will watch the same changes taking place in the body of humanity. When the peripheries are broadened it will be easier to understand the things we never believed in before.

God said: "Let there be light." This is the light that will enlighten. Deepened perception will come with each stage of growth. Verifications in outer form will come every step of the way.

It is not easy to walk a tight rope with a mob shouting beneath. Nor is it easy to maintain rhythm and harmony with the whole world out of step. This is what the chosen few are trying to do today. They have climbed higher poles and strung new wires. They have reached upward, hoping the time will come when all will listen to the fine tonal quality of the new vibration.

We cannot become part of the New Age until we have experienced it within. Talk can go on until doomsday , . . one can hear it shouted from countless platforms, but unless it is born within it will not be a reality without.

In the past few years many have come to an understanding beyond the scope of their training. They have gained knowledge that is impossible to comprehend except through channels beyond the human scope. It may be dangerous to attempt any new venture without knowledge, and the knowledge we need today cannot be found in books. If we are going to experiment with space travel, we must know something about the charting of space. Someone must tread the uncharted paths. In the same way, if we are going to have a space mastery, we must be taught the principles of space mastery. We cannot learn about UFOs merely by observing the strange behavior of the saucers. If they are up there in our skies there must be some means of communication. There must be some way to let us know who they are, and why they are there. Diane has said: "Many will be blessed with the gift of prophecy." We must have rapport before we can be-taught. The voice of the prophet is always heard in the days of travail. Through our prophets we learn something of the roadways ahead. If it were not so we would all be pawns-on the wheels of chance. We would go through cycle after cycle, learning our lessons strictly through trial and error. We would know the penalty of pain with each new forward step.

Many have been readied for channelship since birth. The chosen are equipped with extension cords that can reach out into the cosmos itself. This may seem like something out of the realm of miracles, but it is no more a miracle than the coming of radio and television. Some are capable of developing these extension cords to a point of receptivity; others will not take time to bother or learn.

Revelation is seeing a social necessity and doing something about it. When destruction is on the horizon the need is far greater. If we fail to rise to our personal responsibility, if we fail to take advantage of the opportunities at hand, then the cosmic bill collector steps in and demands his pound of flesh. Change is inevitable. Progress will not be held back. The keener our understanding, the more valuable we are to the life stream that sustains us.

All of this makes sense and is reasonable to the average mind. But understanding cannot be forced. It must come about naturally. It is already apparent in the small groups gathered together in all parts of the world.

Isn't it logical to assume that if the ships have been seen they have been heard from too? Many of the group leaders who were adamant in the beginning have come around to the objective-subjective point of view. They are beginning to become reconciled to the idea that if there is an objective manifestation it is possible there is also telepathic (or some other) communication.

Where are we going to find proof? There is a true adage that tells us "the proof of the pudding is in the eating." First has come the rapid advance in knowledge and understanding that has taken place once channelship was established. Many have gained knowledge beyond a lifetime of ordinary learning in a few short months. Although contacteeism is rejected by the crust of humanity, these open channels are making a major contribution to many departments of life. Scientists and researchers are being forced to look deeper into the matter.

Whether we know it or not, every great change is aided by the intervention of higher orders. We live in the "negatives" until the grooves wear thin. We then switch over to the positive. But there comes a time when there must be a merger with the third principle—for at center we find the point of new creation. In the creative principle we find the answer to growth. We find growth without conflict, harmony without struggle. Life progression becomes a series of mounting glories, and many hitherto unveiled secrets unfold into view.

We are all messengers of the Omnicient One. We have been delegated by the ONE to serve in the capacity best adapted to place and time. We do not have to "shout our wares." The "wares" will do the shouting for us, for the result is ever evident in works.

Alt of this brings us back to the age-old question: Where did man make his first mistake? When we do research in the mythologies and sacred literature we find that man strayed from the mainland when he got off balance. Humanity is like the teeter-totter. We go to one side and then the other. We keep up the pace, teeter-tottering back and forth between extremes until we are finally forced to find the center of the road.

UP RAINBOW HILL

The search for new experience is a thrilling adventure. It quiets the monotony and makes life worth living. Adventure is a hard task master, but a loving one. The adventurer is seldom heralded on his way. Ringing in his ears he hears the admonishing crowd shout: "You're crazy to try it. It can't be done."

The rainbow is the bridge between the visible and the invisible. Perhaps the answer for many will be found in these pages. Others will find it when they are ready to leave the gas bag that we call our world behind them. We're being baited with rewards and countless numbers will find their reward as they go along.

But before we take a definite step forward, we must be able to see where we are going. The evidence must be there before us. The past decade has furnished us with evidential proof. We are certain now that we will one day travel to other planets just as we now fly around the globe. As this new interest develops more devotees will be added. True channels will be opened. The true channel does not wear out. Its traveler does not come to the end of the road. He experiences the joy of a continuous flow, waters as clear and sparkllng as the mountain stream. There are no dams; no blocks. He glides over them and around them.

Many have accomplished the difficult. They are now ready to tackle the impossible. This is the way to bring miracles about. Bring them out of their hiding place, out onto the open highways and byways of life.

UP RAINBOW HILL

CHAPTER THIRTEEN

The heydey of science is here, Many are working against time. They are working with fevered heat. While human status can never be changed in a scientific laboratory, the way it looks now we will change just about everything else. In the great transit, among other things, the human status will be automatically changed. We will not have to use embalming fluids to subdue the decay. The scalpel and the needle will pass into oblivion. We will find more successful ways to turn decaying flesh back to healthy tissue. With a turnabout in physical circumstances there will be proper sustainment, and perfect forms can be brought forth. Nature will attend to that.

This is not a mystic's dream. The pattern is in the forming stage and more and more people are looking in on it. Each day sees added more practical consciousness and greater alerted awareness. Literally millions are beginning to resent the poisons they must consume. They are looking for ways and means to bring our tinseled civilization to an end. With the majority growing cognizant of what is happening to them, the pendulum is due for another swing. Health consciousness will lead that parade. If those who pretend to be our benefactors refuse to destroy the old patterns, the people will. When the creative hierarchies get on the throne (and today they are mounting in numbers), revolutionary changes will be swift and sudden.

Evolution's light is ever burning. It may flicker for a time; it may grow dim. But it is never permitted to be extinguished. Pattern is ever active. It is ever changing. We have a goal today; a goal bigger than we have ever known. When the creators bring forth new patterns, the people honor them with new faith. When we know where we are going, we will whip our horses and drive as we have never driven before.

Will Russia be the motivator behind this mad impetus?

Will they force us to panic into a wild race to the finish line? Rather than looking upon any country as an adversary, as an opponent, why not look upon the change as our own particular challenge ? If Russia is a challenge to our skill, all well and good.

But we must realize that this is no longer a game of competition, but a lesson in cooperation. The time has come to apply our Christian creed to active working principles. The new dispensation means, "Glory to God in the Highest, on Earth peace and good will toward men."

When this creedal form is indoctrinated into the blood streams of humanity; when it can pour from the hearts of people the globe over; when it is exemplified in works, then every single unit will be lifted up.

Exploring the etherian seas means traversing the octaves of space. No one knows just what he will find up there. But we do know the far reaches of space cannot be measured on an Earthly yardstick. We must know how to measure the heights; we must gain some knowledge of the breadth and thickness of the bands we must penetrate. We must also learn something of the tangibility of the various levels reaching to the farthest star. It will be the greatest thrill we have ever experienced, and we can well assess it will be worth the effort we put into it.

Think what it will mean to have the records and histories of other worlds to read! To know that everything we have suffered in this long, arduous cycle has not been in vain; that it has all been preparation for the events to come. A part of the law of life. We will learn, as the prophets of destiny have told us, that the ethers themselves are indestructible. As we have divided our Earth into continents, countries, states and cities, we can expect to find that space has been laid out in its varying dimensions.

Perhaps when we get the idea of distance out of the way the idea of success will not seem so difficult. When Christopher Columbus gave us our own land, he handed us a large plot of rugged terrain to conquer. It was a land strewn with huge boulders, smaller rocks, with virgin timber almost too dense to penetrate. This is the land upon which we have built our homes —our vast empire. When Earthman bored into the subsoil he found minerals, coal and oil. The very materials needed for future building were ready and waiting to be utilized.

Is this something we can anticipate from space? This question helps us to realize that today we stand at another elementary stage in human existence. We have tapped the well-springs of tradition for the last time. The past must be cut off and we must wrap our hopes in the future. Yesterday was a time world. Tomorrow we meet the space world. We must remain stiff-necked in the thought that we dare not look back.

It will take courage to enlarge our spheres of action; the same kind of courage it required for our forebears to build the nation we inherited from them.

To prepare one phase of life for the next is the centuries-old task of our youth. It will be easier for them in this instance for they will have no worthless baggage to discard. They will soon find that they have the resources within themselves with which to accomplish the task. They will tap reservoirs of cosmic strength. Their perceptions will grow keener all the time. With the blossoming of young desire they will drink from the enchanted cup.

All this is bound up in the folds of today's science. Achievements are in the making beyond our wildest dreams. This is the crisis cycle and many individuals will find themselves equipped and wired with extension cords that will reach into the broad sea of the cosmos. Tools will be invented with which to dig into the deep space soil. There will be no further need of the test tube where an element is mixed with another to create something else. Rather we will discover the way to transmute one element into another just as the medieval alchemists claimed to have turned ordinary bricks into gold, perhaps we will find something even more precious when we set out to tap the reservoirs of space. The greats of the past secured their secrets in strong vaults, but the locks can be broken today.

Where will science have its start? Otis Carr believes his new devices will furnish power for automobiles, trains, space ships, hearing aids, portable typewriters —just about everything.

Is free energy the answer?

It could be one of the answers,to be sure. But first we must find a way to absorb the poisons that are now devouring the human race. They may not believe it now, but those who deal in these lethal concoctions will be thankful when they are relieved of their heavy soul burdens. Of what value is a huge bank account, a Cadillac or a mink stole if one cannot enjoy their fruits ? We take dangerous toys from the hands of an infant, but we are afraid to tamper with the menacing playthings of those who still live in an "infant-consciousness." When we find a safer way to recreate the body, with more youthful years added, poisons will be dumped into garbage cans, and science will turn its attention to the life-giving plasmas.

Aligned with destruction, we have become the destroyers. We use the easily available poisons in an attempt to cure our ills.

We have in a measure overcome the sediments of pollution by means of these poisons. We have a bomb spray for everything, even the fleas on a dog. The disease carriers such as mosquitoes and flies no longer are such an awesome menace. But to destroy the horrifics, we have forced our bodies to adapt to the poisons dumped into the atmosphere. Only time will tell how heavy this toll has been on human life.

As Diane has said: "The first task on your planet is the task of cleansing." The United States says: "We have the cleanest country on Earth. How can we improve our state of cleanliness?"

Where are we going to find an element of absorption without resorting to chemical formulas? Perhaps we will find it where Otis Carr believes he has found free energy. We have experimented with everything on the Earth and beneath the Earth, but with the Space Age came our signal to start looking up. Just as we explored the subsoils for the things that have helped build our material greatness,we must now begin to explore the higher ethers in the same way. This means tapping the substances beyond.

Nature works in harmony with color. Diane left with us a set of techniques whereby we might tap "true live color" at Source. We have seen nature's liberal generosity in the green chlorophyll she has given to the leaves of trees. It is shown in nature's grand display of waxen blooms. Color gives a lilt to the soul. It has helped us rise to transcendent heights. But color has not been tried as "the great absorbent." It has not been tried as a screen for the poisons that fill our world. Professor Oswald of Vienna spent twenty years exploring the realm of live color. He made great strides, but he did not find the ultimate.

The time has come to move color forward to its place with New Age methods. The eye will still revel in the shimmering waves of delicate hues; it will continue to enjoy the strange emotional reaction that comes with viewing the spectrum, but color will no longer appertain solely to each organ of the sensorium, but will be utilized therapy—perhaps the greatest "cleanser" we have discovered.

Investigators tells us that color rays act upon certain portions of the brain in the same manner that musical notes act through the nervous fibers. Color vibration might be likened to the undulations of sound thrown into form, while passing along the strings and hollows of musical instruments, when they are being played. Live, vibrating colors can be woven into heavenly patterns, the value of which has never been estimated.

Color therapy is not new to any of us, but color as a means of overcoming the evils let loose in our world is a new concept. I do not merely mean dyes as they are produced in the laboratory, but live color drawn from space.

In recent years fireballs in our skies have been a rather common occurrence. Many believe they have been let loose from so-called spaceships to help clean up radiation in the atmosphere. A few month ago I had the opportunity of seeing one of these huge green fire falls at close range. It was a clear, starlit night as we drove down the freeway leading into desert country. Suddenly I spied a huge green object falling gracefully and rhythmically out of the night skies. We watched for a few moments as it descended toward Earth. About one hundred feet from where we were parked it seemed to elongate into a mass, then fall in huge raindrop, like tears to the Earth. It appeared to be composed of substance comparable to lightweight syrup. But just to gaze upon it for a few moments left one feeling clean and chaste.

How are we going to tap and utilize these bands of color?

This is the dawn of the Space Age. It is a time when all things shall be made new. When we dare to begin something in the larger scheme we soon find that we are part of that larger scheme! In "Over The Threshold," Diane has given a set of techniques whereby color can be drawn from space and used to build a new aural protection against the onslaught of these evils. It is elementary, to be sure, but none of us are yet out of the kindergarten of this realm of new learning.

Hope lies in our potential and new discoveries. Not the byproducts, but fresh originality; that which is pristinely virgin. It has taken centuries of preparation for this new thing to come. Through the years philosophers, religionists and sages have given their lives in the search. Today many of the answers have been chalked on the cosmic blackboard to be read by all. A few have seen not only the light, but its dazzling radiation. Just as the busy sap flows through the branches of a tree, light must shine through the veins of humanity. We are no longer mere creatures crawling over the face of the Earth. We are creators, reaching toward the heavens for the things heaven has to give. Jesus said: "All things are possible in the glorious and eternal now. All things can be changed." All things have been changed.

We have had our spiritual conceptions, now we must find their physical counterpart. If we are to function in the higher realms we will have to use much the same techniques we have used on the lower realms. Towns and cities have been built by individuals working together in group focalization. Group consciousness is the leavening agency necessary to accomplishment. It is time to meet the invisible ones face to face. Perhaps we can do this when we are willing to band together in a unit of power.

Many are feeling the pulse of brotherhood. Those who have had close group association know that in the past few years human potential has broadened and spacial potentials have narrowed so that they have come to a meeting place. The stars and the planets are closer than ever before. We can "feel" them. We know they are there. We have full confidence that on a day soon we will reach the space-shores of other planets. Whether we shall meet superior beings or dragons we do not yet know. We dare not look upon the adventure with fear in our hearts or we are lost.

Science must dig deeper. New sciences must be discovered. Many are convinced that the atom is not the answer. If it were the answer, it would release a stream of purity capable of lifting mankind to the new level. It has not done so, and it obviously never will give us anything but trouble.

Jesus proved to us that we have more than a physical body. He made it plain that we can pass freely from one body to another, When He returned to sup with His disciples He proved that all worlds are interlocked, one with the other. The mineral merges into the vegetable. The vegetable with the animal. The animal with the human. We live in an organic world. We function in an organic body, But a molecular or etheric body is connected to both the physical Earth body and to the body capable of functioning in higher realms. Above and beyond the etheric we have an electronic body. Each body is designed to carry out a certain life function, just as each planet has its planetary function. These bodies might be described as "worlds," each one connected by invisible threads. All are fastened together by the same cohesive substance. When we gain knowledge, wisdom and a practical application of the laws now so completely ignored and so often ruthlessly scoffed at, perhaps we will look back upon Jesus as the great scientist that He was. For the separation and control of the various bodies has been a hopeless enigma to modern man. Even well-studied theologians have skimmed over the Bible passages they did not understand.

By way of further explanation, on the physical level we are confined to a world of cells. Body cells wear out quickly and must be replaced every nine months. This means that every nine months we stand on the frontier of change. As we near the frontiers the frequencies are accelerated. This principle should help us understand what we might expect when we go out into space.

And again it brings us to the enigmatic flying saucer. Perhaps it will be our own behavior pattern that will bring us to a real search for the illusive answers. Recently a young high school student, Sharon Hoag, of El Cajon, California, was given a class assignment to photograph the Moon and its trajectory across the night skies. She used a box camera, leaving the shutter open for about twenty minutes while she played the piano in her father's church. Sharon knew nothing about spacecraft, but when the picture was developed it contained one of the clearest and most convincing saucer photos of all time.

Doris LeVesque of Joshua Tree, California, has many photographs taken of seemingly invisible objects. Doris says she is guided by an unseen hand, and almost without exception her photos will show one or more craft. Others have had similar experiences.

An amateur photographer in Sedgley, England, was photographing the deserted altar of Winchester Cathedral. T. L. Taylor used a .35 millimeter camera equipped with a device to prevent double exposure. When developed, the photograph revealed thirteen ghostly figures in medieval dress.

Mr. Taylor's wife and 16-year-old daughter were present when he took two pictures of the altar. The first showed the choir stalls empty. The second, taken a minute later and five yards farther from the altar, shows the 13 figures, who appear to be standing and kneeling before the 11th century altar. The altar steps are clearly visible through the transparent bodies of some of the figures. The 13 forms were dressed in robes and cloaks of Plantagenet and Tudor times. One is portrayed as bearded, much like the Biblical patriarchs.

This should make us think for a moment what happens when a cellular body is translated into its next highest arc, as in teleportation. The body composed of molecules can become visible or invisible at will. The high frequency process is beyond our comprehension because we cannot see it in operation. The change is instantaneous. It takes place in "the twinkling of an eye." With the transition the new body is like a new-born babe. It must be watched over, cared for, protected from the ever-grasping octopus that is ready to devour it.

The rainbow is the bridge between the kingdoms. The new body is guarded over by a protective band of color and strands of living gold. The area behind and beyond it is overshadowed by a more subtle body, the electronic body. The molecular body appears as an etheric blue, the electronic body is golden. The same threads permeate all bodies; they pervade all life.

The golden ray hangs over us all. It is there for us to use whenever we are ready. When we live in the confines of the "golden circle," we will have attained a spiritual domain.

Just as each individual is wired with the same golden cords, each planet is interpenetrated by the same golden power. It is said that the illustrious Pharoah Amenhotep IV first brought this light to the doorstep of humanity. He told his people there was but one God. All others were His manifestation. The ancient Egyptians were Sun worshippers. Akhnaton, as this king was affectionately called, was one of the True Prophets.

Is it the next great step of science to prove that man is immortal? That he is not limited to this physical body that has been given to him for a little while from the Cosmos itself ? We are fast becoming aware there are new worlds to be explored; that there are new scales of evolution to be reached. Many are beginning to believe that one day life will become a living paradise. When we learn the art of transmutation, when we know that we can transform our bodies without going through the process of destroying them, we will be able to shed light into the souls of man. We will know the true meaning of spiritual illumination. Only a few in any age have known the experience of this chastened ecstasy.

Is it possible to develop all our bodies to a functioning point while still living on this planet ? Nikola Tesla was an electrical wizard. He had merely to command the world of electricity and his commands were obeyed. At the age of 26 he created the electrical transmission system, the source and secret of our world power today. Tesla was well acquainted with the electrical switches in the sky. He could turn these switches on or off with the ease of the ordinary housewife. It is said that high voltage wires held no terror for him. He handled them with the same fearlessness that a child handles a toy pistol. Every cell and every atom was alive with the force over which he had command.

UP RAINBOW HILL

Was Tesla an Earthling or was he a Venusian? Margaret Storm in her book, "The Return of the Dove," maintains that this genius was brought to Earth in a spaceship. She contends that he came as a babe, entrusted to the care of his foster-parents, the Reverend Milutin Tesla and his wife Djouka.

Just as our forebears circumnavigated the globe and our ancestors worshipped at the shrine of images, so we will one day worship at the shrine of "True Reality." We will know that the stars and the planets might one day be our home; that eventually we will mingle with the Children of God and know for a certainty that Life is the never ceasing joy of Immortality.

CHAPTER FOURTEEN

Jesus said: "Ye must be born again." Whether we know it or not the destiny of our Earth hangs on the crux of rebirth. It is said that some 25,000 years ago the cycle began that we are now closing. To be born again in this case means stepping out into another dimension. The worn out shell must be shed as an apple drops its rot. New knowledge is absorbed slowly. It is usually channeled through the medium of the non-conformist, because he has no pre-fixed taboos to discard. He is not steeped in dead traditional cultures.

Our libraries teem with sagas of great men who have lived ahead of their times. The inspired revelations could only be written about them; they must be acted upon now. Some of the wise ones who could look into the future, we revered. Others we scorned. But today, the evolution of awareness makes it easy to accept the most fantastic of yesterday.

We cannot discard our outmoded shell while we still remain chained to the cross of tradition. While we look upon Jesus as our savior, at the same time we depict him as man of sorrows. We fell heir to the crucifixion complex two thousand years ago and we are still nursing it along. We are spilling our lives in ignorance when knowledge and wisdom are ours for the asking. How long will this go on? It will go on until the masses are enlightened. The consciousness of the many directs the few. So long as the masses hang like a weight on our cosmic kite we will not be able to rise to that dimension which has been prepared for us. "I go to prepare a place for you," said Jesus.

Despite scientific opinion, consciousness is essence. While we cannot see it, touch it, taste it, we know it exists. And, as our consciousness is, so are we. Nor can we see with our limited vision the original sublime substance of the first creation. It is everywhere present, buried under a weight of debris we have not been able to lift. This attenuated substance can penetrate and dissipate the dense matter that surrounds us. As we learn how to penetrate, the mists will clear away. Just as we learned how to crack crude oil to make gasoline, and hence power, the substances of the universe can be reduced to the finest essence.

We have split the atom but we have not contacted the essence that lies behind the atom. The creative essence is to be found at the center, the core, of every particle of matter. When it is cast into the furnace of creation, it can be molded by thought into any form we desire to give it. In this way we create and recreate ourselves. We create and recreate our world. In short, we are reborn.

"As each atom is released from its enslaving chrysalis, each central core (the seed) must be returned to a new shell," Diane tells us.

Every kingdom must go through its own life cycle, then enter the next by way of transmutation. Each and every unit of life contributes toward the ultimate end. Man grows as he is able to assimilate. He has come up from the barbarian. He has elevated himself above the savage. There has been a marked change in his physical structure in just one short cycle. Within this century tables groaned with heavy foods; meats and gravies, rich pastries, quantities of goodies to satisfy the most jaded appetites. Today people are growing food conscious. They are watching their calories. This is all part of the plan to change the coarse body to a more refined state.

Tracing back a few years we find one key personality, a non-conformist perhaps, who dared to digress from tradition and plunge ahead of his time. This great man has put the principle to work within the circumference of our own generation. The great Luther Burbank was sired by Father Genius. Like most true creators he was a frail, sensitive lad who in early childhood took his pleasures and his play-time searching for the secrets of the future. Touched by the hand of God, he followed the God-way throughout his long and interesting life.

Luther Burbank realized that all kingdoms are linked together on the same stout thread. He couldn't experiment with human beings but he did experiment with plants. He has often been called the plant developer of this age. There is scarcely a fruit or vegetable coming !o our tables today but what carries the Burbank touch. That his mind was attuned to the higher realms goes without saying. The light from his electronic body shone through every atom of his being. This man is said to have had the keenest vision of any man of our times. His eyes could penetrate into the heart of a flower; into the kernel of the seed; into the veins that ran through the leaves of the tree. He could see with clarity the colors on nature's palette. Often he would stand transfixed as he watched Mother Nature painting colors into her flowers. It is claimed that he could actually see the chlorophyll as it was absorbed into the leaves.

Luther Burbank operated from the plane of "wholeness," not the usual realm of "partness." His extrasensory vision went deep into the germ-plasma itself. His intuitional skill was that of one descended directly from the higher arcs of life. He envisioned the same golden threads running through all plant life which runs through man. In his experimentation with plants, they willingly gave up their most guarded secrets. In plants he found the same divergent strains, the same identical qualities, the same line of evolution, that forms the patterns of all life.

As a little boy he would say, "God told him things." He tuned into the founts of God as we tune in our radio. He drew on the founts of knowledge bringing forth secrets that had not been given to any man of this age. In his consummate research he discovered just how new characteristics could dominate old habits. He learned how new strains became sovereign over the strains that had passed. He selected his seeds with care. He was still more loving in the attention he gave them. His soils were cleansed and sterilized before planting. He used special precautions in transplanting for he knew that at the transition there is a greater degree of fragility. Pests and fungi threatened the life of the seedling just as psychic larvae menaces the life of a new-born babe. To the best of his ability, Luther Burbank made his plants resistant to all attacks.

Early in his venturing he acquired the fine art of hybridizing different species that he might produce an unlimited variety. He discovered there is an affinity in plants just as there is an affinity between human beings. His plants revealed the law of polarities; that there are soul mates in the plant kingdom and that from the mating of these twin-souls new forms are created. He sometimes produced thousands of failures before he found the perfect one. But in dealing with the higher frequencies, his intuition was unerringly accurate. With his keen perception he made the discovery that disease did not attack the perfect germ-plasma. Rather than resorting to sprays and poisons, wherever possible he made his stock immune to attack. By applying the higher laws to the lower Earth, he knew he was doing the creative work that God intended His Earthlings to do.

The keynote of Luther Burbank's success was fresh originality—rebirth in the plant world. He was able to turn the powers of the universe in any direction he dictated. The plant world looked upon him as their God. During his lifetime he developed many new races of parent forms. He mated his flowers and his plants much as a stock breeder mates his prize cattle. He found that whenever there was too wide a departure from affinity a mutation always occurred.

Mr. Burbank found in plant life the divine anthem of creation. He made the discovery that the polarities of male and female must be perfectly balanced if perfect specimens were to be brought forth. That the energies within produce the energies without; that one energy acts upon the other. The care he took with his plants he also administered to his soil. A plant, like human beings, must have the proper environment.

One of this great man's far-reaching feats of genius was his ability to blend the colors in plant life. It is said that he knew more about color than any man of our age. With the color sense of the most talented artist, he mixed his pigments on nature's palette. To him his plants were little people. He treated them as he would like the human specie to treat him . He saw the evolution of man in the making, for had they not come up from the mineral like man? Were they not a part of the same process of growth inherent in all kingdoms?

Mr. Burbank believed that the same principle applied to plants would work in man; that the same undesirable qualities could be weeded out and the best qualities grafted to take their place. He stressed again and again how ravaging fungus destroyed; how it must be cleansed away. Diane has stressed how "psychic fungus" clings to a human being. Is it not the same thing?

Mr. Burbank accentuated adaptation in all of his research. He taught his plants to adapt, and under his guiding hand they took on the shape and quality of their environment. Having clear comprehension of the subtle activities behind all growth, unconsciously, perhaps, he drew forth the essence, the protoplasmic raw material of which all life is created. This he injected into the plants that he loved. Perhaps above all the men of our times he knew that one single drop of this essence contains more power than all the things of earth put together.

There is no question the same basic law that applied to Burbank's creation applies to all life. When we can tap and utilize the Source of all life, we will know the Source of all power. The trinity of evolution, convolution and involution must follow throughout. With the strict observance of this trinity there is no divergence from the mainline.

Octave by octave man has come up through the dungeons of ignorance. He has risen to the heights of materiality. He has touched his exultations; he has wallowed in the mud. Few of us would dismiss lightly the experiences we have lived through, good or bad. Many have risen by the inner sense of call. Others ascended because they were spurred on by that eternal challenge of something greater beyond.

Luther Burbank elevated his inferior stock by blending it with the superior plant life. It wasn't his way to destroy. He never started a war to kill off good and bad because there were too many plants. In his interesting lifetime he blended wild fruits with the domestic variety. He created an environment where the weaker grades could be absorbed by the stronger. Out of this new strains were born. The genius of his creations were sovereign over the old. Realizing they had all come up from the same germinal stream, he knew there was a link of plant brotherhood between them all. As they rose on the ladder of vegetational evolution, to him they became more and more beautiful. He was well aware that all forms go through the same sort of change, that everything on the planet has an ancestral past. All are part of the futuristic stream. Mystics and researchers have known since time immemorial that all germ-plasma must be modified from time to time. That at given intervals extreme and radical changes must be admitted. Such a radical change is on the horizon today.

The history of man is a saga of his cataclysmic struggle to survive. He has resorted to barbarism in the name of conquest. Civilizations have come into being only to vanish forever. Babylon, ancient Egypt, China, Greece; each and every one knew unsurpassed greatness. They reached the heights of their time. And they fell under their own weight. The remnants left for future man were significant to growth. Their symbols were inscribed wherever they thought the symbols would live. Where those civilizations led other civilizations have followed. The pattern has not been altered. We have utilized the best; we have paid tribute to the ruthless methods they used. When we were ready and willing to give our allegiance to those great souls who have guided our footsteps from the depths up to the present time, then we, too, will know the meaning of rebirth.

There have been many trailblazers; many key figures in history. Perhaps some of them were extraterrestrials incarnated to Earth bodies, the same spacemen who are trying to guide our footsteps today.

There are those in every generation who are permitted to glimpse the Charter of the New Age. They have put behind them the things of Earth that they might help turn on the lights of the future. Many are to be found in the scattered groups so recently come into being. They know that the light is trying to shine over our broad horizons. These lights have been extinguished and lighted many times during this long and suffering cycle. But they know too, that the ultimate goal will one day be reached.

The believers are on the ascendancy. Thousands are joining the parade for they know that change is inevitable; the time is up. Everything in our universe will go through the same great change, whether the cells of the body or the cells of the cosmos. All wear a cloak of mortal flesh for a time, but eventually they must slip into their immortal sheaths of finer plasmas.

The fleshy form is a transient tom. It begins with generation and it ends with death. The higher we travel up the scale, the longer we are privileged to live in new bodies. It is believed that some of the planets have a much longer lifespan than ours. They are not subject to the diseases of the flesh. There are no psychological barriers to tear down. Every house, in the beginning, is built of the self-same particles; they are all held together with the same sentient life. If we can use only the changes that have occurred within our own lifetime as a measuring rod, then how can we begin to measure changes that might-take place in a thousand years; a million years, yes even a trillion years? A realization of this time lapse helps us to visualize the wide gap we might meet when we land our craft on other planets.

It is said that our Grand Canyon of Arizona was formed at the time this continent was known as Lemuria. The stone writings unearthed in that area would indicate there has been life on this planet for a long, long time. Those who have traced back the geologic years tell us there is evidence of more than 200,000 years of life. What occurred two hundred thousand years ago? Lemuria has often been called the cradle of the human race. Did extraterrestrials populate the Earth? Have they long since migrated back to their homes in the sky? Perhaps to a planet better adapted to their evolutionary advancement.

All of this will be incorporated in the new time-space foundation. It is the first major move out of bondage toward freedom. At the end of each major cycle, time and space merge, one into the other. Dichotomies give way to trichotomies. This is unity; each domain brought under control by a blending of the best qualities of each. Luther Burbank did it in the plant world. We can do it in the human world. This is the beginning of intelligence.

To solve a problem we must go ahead of that problem. We must embrace a larger periphery. The lesser must be absorbed into the greater. We have lived this entire cycle wrapped up in a chemical balloon. The gases were pure in the beginning but, like any substance that is used again and again, they finally become foul. Today, these putrid gases are escaping; the balloon is disintegrating by way of its own poisons. If we are going to solve today's problems, we must take them to a higher court, a new dimension, a higher arc.

CHAPTER FIFTEEN

It was a day in August, 1935 when two lonely sky wanderers came to their sad end in the cold, dreary tundra of Alaska. That was a day in our century that will never be forgotten. The coast line from Alaska to California was bathed in a heavy fog, the last requiem to a man beloved by all the world. Skywriters were busy inscribing a final chapter in the life of a great chieftain, America's ambassador of good will, Will Rogers.

I recently visited Claremore, Oklahoma, where all that was mortal of the wise, rope-slinging cowboy reposes and is at rest. Just to stand there before his mammoth statue gave me a comfortable feeling that this man left this world with all his sums finished. Will had fulfilled his major obligations. He had paid his debts. He had achieved his life's ambition. It was as if an unseen hand had guided the stick of that little red bus; an unseen hand that led two intrepid adventurers, Will Rogers and his pal Wiley Post, out into a newer and greater event. Will was still wearing the laurel wreath that would help him press on to greater goals. It is an Indian tradition to reach for the Sun. He had found his Sun, beyond the visible horizon.

There was a prayer in my soul as I paid tribute to Rogers, whose simple word was mightier than the sword. His one secret was now etched into the hard metal of the imposing statue. It was part of his own illuminating personality; the password to the throne of nations. It read "I never met a man I didn't like."

Early in life Will Rogers had discovered the well-spring of brotherhood. He was the biggest brother to all nations that this century has known. His sense of fellowship for every man came from the deep folds of himself. He could see something of worth, find something to love, in every man he looked upon. The riches Will recognized were the values that could be weighed on the scales of heaven. He said many times that possessions could not bring happiness until one learned how to use possessions. He was aware also that the best in world leadership could not break the chains of woe, but that simple souls, the prophets and the saints could chase away man's gloom. It made little difference to Will Rogers who a man was, or where he was born. He was a human being, and Rogers liked him. If the person came from the heaven world or another planet, if he was capable of starting a chain reaction for good, Will was for him.

There are many unadorned souls like Rogers in the world today. They are filled to the brim with goodness. With preordained design they have come to open the new vistas. Will Rogers was a rough-and-ready, gum-chewing man who believed that good humor made relatives of everybody. Perhaps he did more to cement friendships between man and nations than any man since Abraham Lincoln. He proved to the world that wit linked with wisdom can crack the highest walls of rancor. He knew that the brotherhood of man is not something to attain to, that it lies sleeping in the heart and soul of every human being.

From boyhood Rogers had had a healthy outlook on life. He had a wholesome outlook on world affairs. It was the ideal that he worked for. He believed that if all men could look at life as he did there would never be occasion for war.

Such men as Will Rogers are the healers of the ills of mankind. They serve good humor instead of champagne. When we can laugh at life and with life, we know how wonderful life can be.

Why is man on earth? This question has been asked down through the ages. Perhaps the answer is to be whole and complete within himself, to experience in some measure every phase of existence. The sages tell us that earth is a school where we must learn our lessons. Little by little we are taught how to be free, not with a false freedom, but with a freedom that is enduring and immortal.

To be free one must build an aura free of psychic larvae that eats eternally at our entrails. We need something to prevent us from sucking in the flotsam that is part of our vermin filled world. As we wipe out one menace, it seems we always do something to bring about another.

If Will Rogers were alive today he would tell us that war must go; that poverty must go; that the things that create a menace must be wiped out?

We have been conditioned to false concepts. We haven't learned to discriminate between the false gods and the real. Perhaps Will Rogers looks down upon us from time to time. Bemoaning the state of affairs on earth he once said: "There is no country in the world where a person changes from hero to goat and goat to hero as they do with us. It's not our public men you can't put your finger on, it's our public. We don't know what we want, but we're always ready to bite somebody to get it."

Throughout his life Rogers harbored a secret hurt in his heart for the wrongs imposed upon his people, the Indians. He had always taken immense pride in his Red Brothers. He often said: "They didn't come over on the Mayflower. They met the boat." Will was a champion roper, but he always threw the rope so that nobody would get hurt. If he could talk to us from beyond the spheres of earth he would tell us that we cannot have friendships until we know how to be friends.

Men like Will Rogers are the saviors of civilization. We need more of them. Harmony was the keynote of his life. Harmony is to be found at the center of all things. Our present ideologies have seemingly revealed the worst rather than the best in us. Now we must pull ourselves up by our own boot straps.

The new era was heralded in by spectacular histrionics. There will be many new and exciting acts in this drama before the curtain comes down again. The world is asking, what will these changes be like? None of us know the whole truth, and perhaps the maddest fiction would not be able to tell us. Diane has said: "Once the goal is in view, Earth beings will go in throngs to find their paradise."

We can start this great work by listening to the voices from afar; by opening our hearts to the needs of others; by helping to bring in the age of brotherhood in all ways that we can. We have been told this brotherhood exists on other planets. We have been told it is the root and fiber of their greatness and stability. Will Rogers had the answer when he said: "I never met a man I didn't like."

We are a people who live in our environment for good or for bad. Only when we can see a better system in operation will we believe.

Many have asked if the ships be atom fueled? We have looked to nuclear energy as our great hope, but there are those who believe that fate has handed us hemlock to drink in the form of atoms. Perhaps we will still find the transforming qualities or something that can be turned into a real virtue in the atom. But it remains to be seen. Any new thing has two sides; the positive and the negative. Nuclear energy tis great power. This has been demonstrated. If a constrictive side can be found without its dire aftermath, then it will go on to further greatness. Our scientists have their ears attuned to the earth. They are burning midnight oil trying to expand their perceptions into broader fields. Will our progress be more rapid when we meet these extraterrestrials face to face? Will it change the style of our living? We can only wait on the sidelines—wait, look and listen.

But without harmony nothing big is going to happen to us. Just as harmony must be established in individual relationships, it most be established in the hearts of nations. Our earth's premise has been one of wide diversity. We've called it freedom, and it has been freedom of a sort. Will Rogers puts it this way: "If Russia wants a statue of liberty we will loan her ours. Ours has its back turned on us at the present time. Every politician talks about Lincoln, but none of 'em ever try to imitate him."

In our country we have been allowed to deviate from the norm by believing that the tree must have its many branches. In religion this diversity has created a multitude of sects. Each one claims to have "the last word of God." The same is true in science, philosophy and art. Each has placed its own hierarchy on the throne.

Epochal history lies before us. Expanding potentialities are there to be tapped. First we must be tested. As Plato said: "Leaders must be tested until they are like pure gold." Those who take their seats in the new affairs must be made worthy of their responsibility. If there is a spark of perfection, it must be found for progress is dependent upon how we start. The new civilization must be set in motion. It must start with the spirit of brotherhood, and with a sincere humanitarian gesture.

Will Rogers said : "Everybody's got a scheme to set the world right again. You can't fix the affairs of the world, but you can go back and find the mistakes and try to fix 'em. Civilization hasn't done much but make you brush your teeth."

We need Will Rogers today, or we need more like him. Only a man with compassion for his fellows can serve with wisdom and humility. We need men who are honest, open and frank; men who have achieved a measure of immortal consciousness.

"Some folks do sums with figures," said Will, "Sometimes they get good at it, too. Like this fella Einstein. Then some folks do sums with words. I did my sums with humor." He did it that way because he never met a man he didn't like.

UP RAINBOW HILL

CHAPTER SIXTEEN

The great federation of saucer movements has done a great deal toward bringing a feeling of unity among peoples. Thousands are donating their time and their efforts toward this great good. They know that we are at the end of the road and that a reconstruction program is necessary. We cannot go much farther without learning something more of universal laws. But we must immediately learn a great deal more than we now know about interstellar space.

Let me repeat again that in the beginning the majority of the saucer groups were formed to investigate the sightings. This was the original purpose and it was a necessary prelude to a working base. Many did a marvelous job alerting the people to what was happening. Without the sighting era we would have gone nowhere at all.

Today a sighting means virtually nothing. The sighter is excited for a few moments but the next morning it is forgotten. Sightings alone have proved nothing. A few years ago "Flying Saucer Review" by far and wide the best saucer news medium, started out strictly as a sighting organ. Derek Dempster, an RAF pilot and admittedly a "nuts-and-bolts" man, was the editor. But since the magazine's inception he has had a change of mind. In a recent issue he said:

"Ever since I became interested in the flying saucer enigma, I have cherished the feeling that the UFOs are as solid as the Russian's Sputniks, the American Explorers, or a big, red, double-deck London bus. But through the last four years the strangeness of certain sightings, coupled with a number of incidents utterly divorced from UFOs led me to a reappraisal of the facts, and subsequently to the conclusion that they are as I have imagined them, but that there is a clue to their behavior in a number of manifestations that people would call plain supernatural.

"Early in 1954," Dempster wrote, "one of the test pilots of the French Fouga Aircraft Company in Pau, in the Lower Pyrenees, reported approaching the aircraft he was piloting, an unidentified flying object hovering near the town, but that he was forced to turn away because of the intense heat which built up in his cockpit.

"About two months later, a United States Air Force Starfire was scrambled to intercept an unidentified flying object picked up on the American radar defense chain. The key fighter made a successful contact, but the crew bailed out because the cockpit became unbearably hot.

"In the Norwegian incident, Trygvie Jansen, a master painter, was driving home one evening after work when he was suddenly confronted with a flying saucer hovering over the road. It was an amazing sight but even more extraordinary was the tingling sensation experienced as he watched. But the greatest shock was yet to follow. When he got home he found his car had changed in color from beige to dark green.

"The Irish Sea story involved the trawler Ella Hewett, which in November, 1957, was overflown by a very bright object reported by many eyewitnesses ashore. The peculiar fact about this incident was that on the following morning the bridge of the trawler appeared to have been stripped of its white paint. Only the red-lead undercoat appeared to have remained. And yet, on the day after, the bridge was back to its normal resplendent white. It had changed overnight."

The "tingling sensations" seem to be a part of the strange experiences of many who have seen UFOs in the skies. Contactees have stated their experiences have been preceded by "tingling" in the body. A few moments prior to my own strange 1939 experience in the flames, this tingling sensation overwhelmed me like a violent earthquake. The visitations of Diane have been heralded in by the same sensations. Before the transfiguration episode at Fontana, California, my body took on intense heat. And from the antics of my little dog, Kim; she, too, must have had something of the kind happen to her.

I recall this same strange heat on another occasion when an odd-looking key was placed in my hand. It is said that a key is verification of true contact. As the key touched the palm of my hand it was accompanied by an electrical shock that brought tears to my eyes,

Again quoting from the Dempster article:

"The trouble with mankind is it is 'tone-deaf' to all but a few of the octaves of nature, and like a two-dimensional creature trying to comprehend a three-dimensional animal, quietly says to itself of anything its mind cannot understand: 'There ain't no such animal.'

"There are more such animals in existence than we can ever hope to know about for the time being," he concludes. "And there are forces which our descendants will become aware of as they continue to evolve. And these are the forces it seems the flying saucer designers have learned to tap and the crew to manipulate."

People have looked to their governments for the answer. Thousands of dollars of the taxpayers' money have been spent in futile investigations. So long as we attempt to measure another dimension on our worn out yardstick, the answers will continue to evade us. When we are willing to open our ears to great learning; when we are ready to make an effort to understand these universal laws, then that which we call supernatural will become natural phenomena.

The concerted effort of the many saucer groups will help bring this about. We are all linked together in a chain of relationships. In my first years of training by an unseen monitor I was forced to use conceptual words as a means of running up and down the scales. I was shown how to run them up to the highest scale of understanding then down the scale to the lowest point they would reach. I soon found the point of relationship, the way they linked up with all the other words in the human vocabulary.

The tremendous importance of the small groups now being formed cannot be ignored because of their worth and value as a whole. The day has come when one man spearheading a campaign is not enough. Not even a Will Rogers could stand up under the vicious barrage. These little groups, dedicated to healing and growth, can in a measure serve as a bulwark against the evils that have invaded us. Their consciousness can do a great deal toward keeping the balance.

Since the coming of strange ships, these groups have been springing up like mushrooms. About a year ago, Major Wayne Aho, retired, of the United States Marine Corps Intelligence, took up the banner. He has induced thousands to become part of this great band. Major Aho has been tireless in his efforts. No hours have been too long; no part of the work too difficult.

In their short lives, some of these groups have grown to good size. Others have remained little hubs, but hubs of devotion. Most of them have graduated from the sighting class and are now anxious and waiting for the next move forward. These people know that the new era is here and that we cannot fly back to our little cocoon this time. If we can remain devoted to something we have not seen, whether Doctor Jung's "mythical savior" or spacemen, then we can become good servitors. Many who have never seen a UFO believe just as strongly as those who have seen dozens of them. They are just as sincere in their devotion; just as adamant in trying to evaluate , equate and understand. Once they become an integral part of a group, the group itself expands.

The consciousness contributed by these small gatherings might never be properly measured in the world of average men. From them is issuing the fuel of inspiration which should help to bring in the new things of the future. Many go to bed at night as the same individual they have been since birth. They wake up in the morning completely changed. Something has happened to them. Their minds have expanded. They tingle with new energies. They are alive and ready for flight. Something new has been etched into their consciousness. Dozens have asked me the same question: "Do you think I have made contact?"

But no one can answer, for there is yet no factual answer to their questioning. Perhaps it means another of Earth's children has been awakened from a centuries old slumber. The first certainty he embraces is the fact that it is no longer one Earth but the whole universe. He sees all as part of the absolute , the whole. He knows oneness with all things. He also knows he has placed one foot in paradise and he will not be content until both feet are across that evanescent borderline.

Perhaps at no time since the early days of Christianity have human beings been so completely devoted to a cause. A recent saucer convention sponsored by the San Francisco Bay Area groups brought people from far and wide. They stayed until the last speaker was heard. These people were not supporting a mirage, but the greatest reality of our age.

Many who have become members of groups are serving despite the fact that they are not aware of their service They seem to be following some deep urge from within; a feeling rather than a knowing. Often they are indiscriminate in their loyalties. They shout their enthusiasm to their neighbors when they should hold their tongues. For the neighbor's time has more than likely not yet come. In time all will partake of the same revelation. Those who have held fast to a belief in miracles are now looking eagerly toward their performance. These are the days they have earnestly prayed for. They stand ready and waiting for their own apocalypse.

Once they become a part of group focalization there is no more doubt in their minds. It is no longer an idle dream. The whole picture becomes as scientific as the most down-to-earth science. It is no longer a question of "it might be." Rather, it is a matter of when and how.

It is said that if the mind can embrace a concept long enough, it can eventually bring it to pass. The consciousness generated during the past ten years will one day bear rich fruit. Many already feel the foreshadowing of things to come. They feel the approach of new events. They experience flashes of inspiration they cannot explain.

These small groups are serving as a vortex; the womb of generation. The adherents are drawn from every bracket of human society, yet all work together in harmony. They exhibit the same enthusiasm and the same devotion to an almost phantasmic cause.

Throughout history it has been the same. The early Christians were devout, yet they knew not where they were going. They were ready to brave death at every turn that they might spread the message,

The fact remains that the greater the cause, the greater is the expansion that is needed. In our long histories we have not strayed far enough from home base. We have never followed so nebulous a trail. The dedicated ones feel they have nothing to fear. If the beings from space had intended to wreak havoc upon it, they could have won the battle without a struggle. Rather, it seems all too evident that they have come to show us how to sublimate and transmute our woes. So why not give them a helping hand? Will Rogers would have done so. The greats of our age will be happy to clasp their hand in friendship. Thousands are ready to open the doors of hospitality. They will be entertained royally, for we will look upon them as royalty.

CHAPTER SEVENTEEN

Through the centuries world libraries have been filled with books and periodicals about subjects existing as yet only in the minds of the authors. Many of these written records have served to stimulate greater interest, but few have been a proving ground for facts. The theories furnish the seeds for the facts to come later.

The seeds of the New Age have been sown again and again. But like the curious city gardener planting seeds for the first time, he usually digs them up before they have time to sprout. We have prepared the soil. We have planted the seeds, but again and again they have been dug up before they have had time to flower and fruit.

These are cosmic times. We have come up against the bar of justice and it must be acknowledged. We are facing issues of cosmic importance. If we are going to participate in this golden drama, we must become golden within ourselves Many are putting their toes on the ladder. Many are beginning to view the picture from a new vantage point. They want to glimpse the beautiful scenery of the higher worlds before they decide to enter. We are rising to a new octave. Each note must harmonize with every other note. In time we will create a new scale. We will reach the chords that are connected with the music of the spheres.

We are in the midst of the greatest drama since the birth of Christ. But this time the virus in humanity's bloodstream must be cleansed. One asks: "Why haven't I been told these things before? Why have I been blinded to these beautiful realities?"

Minor cycles creep up on us slowly. Minor cycles are all part of the preparation for the major changes. Through the centuries only a few have had the key to the mysteries. They have stayed in their caves On High, giving their lives casting our inspiration to the worlds beneath. Many times we have come up to the bar but, like the breaking waves on the shore, it has vanished before we could capture it.

This time it has been halted as though suspended by threads from the heaven worlds. The evolutionary life that has moved sluggishly along for centuries has suddenly spurted forward.

At given intervals nature brings out her brooms, her brushes and her mops to help with the clean-up job. She usually takes a small portion at a time; one part of the Earth will be buried under snow and ice. Another portion will be seared by blistering heat and hurricane-force winds. Now and then a flash flood will drench part of the Earth, bringing devastation in its wake. Approximately once each century, the Earth goes through a complete cleansing. One such event occurred in November of 1833 when the stars literally fell upon our heads. I quote from the pen of the late Professor Omstead of Yale University:

"Those who were fortunate enough to witness the exhibition of shooting stars on the morning of November 13, 1833, probably saw the greatest display of celestial fireworks that has ever been seen since the creation of the world. The extent of the shower of 1833 was such as to cover no inconsiderable part of the Earth's surface. This is no longer to be regarded as terrestrial, but as celestial phenomena, and shooting stars are no longer to be viewed as casual productions of the upper regions of the atmosphere, but as visitants from other worlds, or from other planetary voids.

"This was a day of days. The whole heaven seemed to be in motion and suggested to some the awful grandeur of the image employed in the Apocalypse upon the opening the sixth seal when the stars from heaven fell upon Earth. "And the stars of heaven fell upon Earth, even as a fig tree casteth her untimely figs when she is shaken by a mighty wind."

It is said that, following this shower the atmosphere was clean and pure as it has never been before. The story of the "shower of the stars" has a personal connotation, for I remember vividly that as a little girl of five I was taken to visit two elderly maiden ladies called "the Tracy sisters." Their mother had witnessed this shower. I was allowed to hold in my little hands a fragment of one of the fallen stars. It is a picture that has remained in my memory always, although other events of that period have completely vanished from my mind. Perhaps it was destined to serve as a reminder that one day I would be writing about the stars and other planets; that I, too would become a messenger to Earth.

Prophecy is not predicated on seership. It is the ability to follow the golden threads out into the Great Unknown. Those who are capable of looking into the future stand as the sturdy oak against the storms of time. Today with the veneer of civilization wearing away, we are seeking a more durable coat of paint, But most of us are aware that it goes deeper than that. The termites have eaten into our structure until it will no longer take merely another coat of paint.

We have had our warnings. We are being warned today. The siren will continue to wail until the very eve of destruction. The greatest danger lies in our enormous stockpile of atom bombs stored over the face of the Earth. What we store, we must eat, or else it leaves behind its stench of decay. We have stored much for our day of destruction. Only a miracle can save us. Each wave of violence brings us closer to the final tide that will wash us from the face of the Earth. We have signed a pact with the devils of destruction and it is going to be difficult to escape the penalty of that pact.

Destruction is a powerful magnet. Without warning it pulls us down into the fiery furnace. Construction rides the air waves on invisible wings. It lifts us ever upward. While each end of the pole serves its own specific purpose, one tiny mistake on the part of a thoughtless person can set off that nuclear stock-pile and finish us as Earthlings forever.

We smashed the atom to increase our knowledge, but was fission developed at the price of wisdom? Throughout this long cycle we have crept

through the dark. We've taken the bumps one after the other. But what were the bumps of the past compared to our present atom bomb stockpile? This time we dare not venture a single footstep in the dark. No mere meteoric shower, but a mushroom of gorgeous fireworks as lethal as the
devil's playground would greet such a step.

We usually look upon novelists as dabblers in fiction; the children of God fired with a fabulous imagination. But many times in our history fiction has proved eventually to be as true as fact. The Jules Vernes have come with us all along the way. Today perhaps another Jules Verne has appeared on the scene in the personality of that charming English author, Neville Shute. This man, in a quiet manner, has placed his pen of power upon the pages of a book entitled "On the Beach." It is a trenchant message of what could and might happen to us. The book could turn out to be prophetic history. In his own distinctive style, Mr. Shute is letting us know just what might happen to this stockpile of bombs.

Perhaps we might go a notch further than Mr. Shute. If the end of the age is close at hand, the swing of the pendulum is still to be considered. One day it swings to the left, the next to the right. If enough people over the face of the globe have the courage to stop the pendulum when it reaches center, we will find the door that will lead us to safety. Transmutation is an alien word to most of us. It means bringing the fire from heaven to burn out the dross, then changing our garments from the scanty attire of the burlesque performer to that of a monarch of spirit.

From all appearances the weight of evidence is on the side of disaster. We're going around in a mad dream. With the threat of the Earth being stilled by atom bombs, this is no time for the dreamer. The Earth could be laid fallow for a thousand years. Some scientists estimate that it would take at least that long for the radiation poisons to dissipate.

In the meantime, what is to become of the countless numbers who have worked to prevent this horrific? Will they too be forced into oblivion along with the malevolent destroyers?

Since each round of evolution is complete within itself, it must have its beginning and its climax. There are always those caught up in the evolutionary round who must go on ahead. Somewhere along the line they have earned the right. Likewise, a planet comes to the end of another long term. Archeology and geology are replete with change. The face of the Earth has been altered many times by floods, ice glaciers, and other cataclysmic events. When human consciousness grows in debauchery to the point where human beings can no longer live in their filth, then something must come to kill out every last vestige of the scum and slime that has been created.

When we turn to the atom we have a wildcat by the tail. We cannot hide our world treasures this time. They will stand as we left them when our bodies turn back to dust. They will remain until time eventually releases them back to their source.

This time we are trapped in our own cage. Only a miracle can offset the debacle. If bombs are dropped on New York and in turn on Moscow, the entire world will be drawn in. The poisons let loose will travel to every nook and cranny. None can escape. The curtain will come down and the theater of Earth will be locked up perhaps for many centuries.

What will become of the millions of beings who live on Earth? No one can say with any degree of certainty. It is a mute question as to whether the molecular body will be destroyed along with the cellular body. We cannot yet estimate the force of that ghastly weapon. It would mean the end of human existence. The essences out of which we are composed would go back to their founts for a long, long rest.

Again, it could be that there will be another major exodus as in the days of Moses. Would ships come down from the skies to take those who are ready, those who have been willing to look and listen? It is claimed by some contactees that countless numbers of ships are already high in our skies. "Behold He cometh with clouds; and every eye shall see Him, and they also which pierced Him; and all kindreds of the Earth shall wail because of Him."

The warriors who have lived for conflict must be cleansed of their scourge. Throughout the cycle, they have been as vultures feasting upon humanity's liver. What will become of them when the dust of the bombs has passed?

While they have been sinners, in their hearts and souls they have believed in their cause. War was in their blood, their bone and their sinew. They knew of no other way to gain peace except by way of war. Perhaps a place has been prepared for them, too. A place where they can be cleansed and purified. As the vibrations are changed, conditions will change. Transition will come but it need come through death and destruction only if we force it to. It can come through transmutation and regeneration, also. In war we use the fire of cannon and bombs to maim and kill. In transmutation we use the fire of Divinity to cleanse, purify and uplift. One is the way of war; the other the way of peace.

CHAPTER EIGHTEEN

We have climbed to the heights. We have tilled the lands from ocean to ocean. Now we must learn how to till the super-soil of space. We live to grow, we grow to live. Higher and higher we rise through the upper spirals of consciousness. At the base of each new horizon we must have a larger foundation. At the portal of each change we are given two ways to go. We can take the left hand path or we can take the right. The left hand path means fighting our way through. It is a path frustrated with struggle. If we take the right hand path and ignore the left, then we are apt to become overbearing tyrants; an accentuation of the positive over the negative. All life, even the tempestuous elements, will step aside to let the man pass who is determined to stay in the middle road.

We need not worry as to how it will be accomplished. When we make up our minds that it can be done, the help will be there. Perhaps our inter-planetary friends will be there, too. This is the purpose of telepathic channelship. It is the purpose of contact evidence in advance of landings. Many are beginning to live in a paradise thought world. As the groups are knitted together there will be greater understanding.

Are we ready to abandon our old gas bag? Is it time to start putting clean essences into the new one? Getting rid of the old and adopting the new will be a thrilling experience, but individual effort is too slow. In unity is strength and security. With the opening of space doors will come opportunities beyond anything we have ever known. How we enter will determine what we will achieve. We're casting our rod into unknown waters, and we're casting in the dark. That is why we must learn to "tap" in, "tune" in or receive messages in any way possible.

This is not a new thing in the experience of mankind. The day this Earth cycle began we had to go through the same thing. We began in darkness, then came the dawn, and suddenly the sunlight of our materialistic day. That was a long time ago. It is not easy to translate the experiences of a long cycle into terms we understand. For this reason we must give our best efforts to scientific research. There is no time for selfishness; no time to think how much money is in it. When disaster comes upon us we will be forced to act as one.

In time of distress the social matron fraternizes with the housemaid; the bank president with the garbage collector. This is banding together, all speaking the same language. All have the same sympathies. When human beings are moved by a common objective they act as one. The chain will be forged eventually. But it means the development of new techniques, new methods, new ideas. They must all be drawn from the realm of true principle.

The speeding up processes of the past fifty years have been preparing us for our trek into space. Before the days of the automobile people remained in the same region from cradle to grave. Parents willed the home to their children; it was left to the grandchildren, and on through the generations. This is fixation. If it were not for the introduction of new patterns we would warp and decay. New environment awakens new interest. New enthusiasms lead the way ever onward and upward.

When we learn how to translate the substance of cell life into the powerful molecular life, we will then be able to change with the speed of light. Many who pass from the body at death will translate immediately to another dimension. They will not touch the already overflowing astral realms.

As we creep toward the edge of time we know we must face these changes. It is no longer a dream; the "New Age" is here. Diane has said: "The Earth is entering a new phase. We must be prepared to go along with it."

We found the treasures of our Earth plane by boring into the earth. We found it when we removed layers of solid mass of substance. We will find the values of the higher planes by penetrating into the sky-blue ethers. We will find oil there,too; not the heavy, sticky substance we refine into gasoline, but a lubricant that will help us loosen the hard concretions which cling to us like barnacles.

Perhaps we will find gold and precious gems there too; that which is golden buried deep in the hearts of men. There will be gems brilliant with luminosity, gems that have not been adulterated by greed and selfishness. These are the treasures for which we have searched; the treasures we shall find.

The power of magic is in us all. It needs merely to be called forth. It is easier to call it forth today than at any time in our existence. We have come up through a cruel barbarism, but in it we have slowly ascended the scales. Civilization has endowed us with a certain refinement. The pure at heart have lived as neighbor with those who were unclean and have helped to make them clean.

When we climb the heights we will be able to look back into the depths. One who has attained to cosmic awareness can view all points at once. We will be cosmic citizens when we learn to live in the cosmos and when we know the cosmos lives in us. Here all things are related and time and space merge into one.

The more ponderous the matter, the greater the density. Today we are buried under our own weight. To measure the whole by its parts is to become lost in the "partness" of things. We live in a so-called three-dimensional world but we know little about the third dimension. The fourth interpretates the fifth on up until the golden threads reach the seventh dimension. If we could touch the seventh dimension for one brief moment, we would know the meaning of spiritual illumination. We would experience the unity and complete awareness which exists throughout all God's universe. Few have had this true experience. Few have come to that point where the mind of man and the mind of nature meet. In the days ahead more and more will be taken to that dimension. They will experience perceptions keener than anything we have ever known before. In time there will be many more channels. More will be added to the fold. This is the way of transmutation rather than the rod of force.

Just as changes take place in our world, the pollution and waste can be cleansed from the aura of the Earth. The auric body acts as a bulwark against invasion. When perceptions are refined, matter is refined. When matter is reduced to its finest point, the lowest and more virulent substances must give way to the higher essence. Major changes are brought about first through the inner. Then they are made manifest outwardly. As the lower reaches upward, the higher descends and eventually they meet at center.

We have stumbled along through life when we might have ridden in golden carriages. With all the white heat of our emotions we have been too lazy to come out of our comfortable shell. Inertia has claimed us because we have not known how to be rid of the heavy coating of pollution that has clung to our aura.

During the last half century inertia has set in in earnest. It has lulled us into a Rip Van Winkle sleep.

As vibrations are lifted we reach to greater heights. Changes in the upper arcs are rapid; on the lower arcs they are slowed down. As Diane has said: "Many from higher planets elect to come to Earth, sometimes in Earth bodies, sometimes by adaption."

What becomes of them, swallowed as they must be in our Earth's pollution? It is reasonable to suppose that some would be lost, for the process of osmosis is the same on all planes. It is said of evil: "We first endure; then embrace." Our bodies become the product of what we eat and what we breathe. An extreme "sensitive" might soon become an unwitting victim of our dirty Earth. In time he might forget his heritage. He would become the victim of environment. To live on Earth would require a solid body, a prison from which it would be hard to escape. Just as the lung fish adapted to land, this physical body would be supplied him in time, but with it would come the vicissitudes of Earthly living.

It is this density we must think about when we ask the questions: "Why don't they land in numbers? Why are they so illusive? Why do they not make themselves known to us?" If we will stop and think a moment, the answer is crystal-clear. Perhaps they have not been in our environment long enough to make this adaptation. Their bodies are not sufficiently concrete to withstand a prolonged sojourn. This was made apparent through Diane. Like the Defied Ones, she could come in her subtle quasi-body, but such a body cannot be maintained in the Earth's vibration for any considerable time. As a consequence they are looked upon as supernatural. When people do not understand the supernatural, they categorically deny the existence of other worldly beings.

If each planet has its own individual density, its own special frequencies, we, like our visitors, would first have to learn to adapt to new vibrations when the final breakthrough comes. If one has had the rare experience of traveling into space in his subtle body, he knows that the amplification is beyond words to describe. It is beyond our ability to depict because it has no Earthly definition.

As density falls away, leaving a body fashioned of rarified substances, that body is without its protective armor. It is without flesh and bone. Every least sound is comparable to the pounding in a boiler factory; a battery of hypnotic drums beating on the door of the mind.

Again, let us swing the pendulum to the other extreme. As one makes his adaptation to the higher vibrations he penetrates deeper and deeper into the archives of knowledge. The peripheries of the mind are broadened. Cosmic verities are balanced. Intelligence is assimilated at this extreme just as ignorance has been absorbed at the other. This is the way we grow. It is the path of wisdom. It is also the road downward to decay. The entire universe is relative. We "live and move and have our being" in a universe of relativity.

Spirit descends into matter. Matter is assimilated by spirit. In space we find the balance wheel. Perhaps we must go off on tangents at times so that we might better appreciate the main line once we find our way back. We go off on tangents to specialize rather than to universalize. We cannot measure the heights by the abyss, nor car we measure the abyss by the heights. In chemistry one element is changed into another. In alchemy we transmute one element into another. Each has its own weight, length, breadth, and thickness. As one scale is finished, there are many more dimensions to be mastered in the dizzying heights. We climb one rung at a time, going from time to space, and from space to the "absolutes." We begin from the Earth premise in a physical, cellular structure we call a body. As it rises it is refined into a molecular body; the molecules held intact in an electronic body. All are interchangeable. All are part of the one.

Why haven't we been told this before? We have, but we haven't listened. Today is no different from yesterday. The people would not believe Edison or the Wright brothers. The same know-it-all snickers have accompanied every revolutionary happening since history began. History is punctuated with change, but the world never changes of its own free will. Conquest by force will not win for us this time. A good portion of the Earth might be blasted away before the ignorant wake up.

We are all part of one Great whole. The substance out of which man is made existed before he came into being. The substance that built our world will have existence when the world passes away. We are all linked together on one long chain. We are as close to each other subconsciously as breath itself. When we stop fighting and try living together in brotherly affection, then we will soon forget that war has ever existed on this planet; that the discords upon which we thrived were only experiences we had to go through to learn our lessons.

There is no escape. All avenues of retreat are blocked. The atom bomb has done something we could not have done without it. Now we can go up or we can go down; we can take our choice. One day we shall be forced to shed this body of cells just as the Earth will shed its hard encrustations. Time will take care of that. In immortality alone shall we find permanence.

Highly evolved beings can live in a cellular body and a molecular body simultaneously. They can shift from one to the other in a flash materialization and dematerialization, as we call it. Throughout history many have found the secret. They have traveled the uncharted paths while still inhabiting a physical body. Now, with universalization expanding, many more will be able to do the same. They will discover in a moment of time they can transfer their consciousness from one body to another.

There is an up and a down, also a middle path. This is an indestructible principle that belongs to the Law of the Absolute. Specialization without universalization leads to a fatalistic end. We have reduced our world to an atom, now we must expand that atom to God.

CHAPTER NINETEEN

It we take the time to read the road signs along the pathway of life, we know that the changes ahead surpass anything we have laced before. To be sure, we do not know the way, and we are not going to find the path unless we are willing to go adventuring. It is futile to attempt to put pencils to work as we would with a problem in simple mathematics. We must depend in this case upon true guidance. This does not mean the pedagogic interpretations of man gleaned from books, but inspirational guidance and direction from the spheres beyond Earth.

The human family has come up through the fathomless depths of time. Each life stream had witnessed the pageantry of the ages. All are in agreement that love is the ultimate of all things. When we learn how to love, we learn how to live. Every soul is reaching out for that something or that someone who can help us bring forth the perfect creation.

Sacred, ancient teachings tell us that back in the night of time, man was an androgynous being; that the two sexes, male and female, lived in one body. "The Lord caused a deep sleep to fall upon Adam, and he slept; and he took one of his ribs and closed up the flesh instead, thereof. And the rib, which the Lord God had taken from man, made he a woman, and brought her unto man. And Adam said: 'This is now bone of my bones, flesh of my flesh; and shall be called Woman because she was taken out of Man."

The doctrine of "twin souls" can be found in the folds of all older literature. When complements meet there is instantaneous recognition. The expression of the masculine and feminine ray is complete. But on their journey through the cosmos each must travel its divergent path until the time comes for reunion. This same principle is in evidence throughout nature.

It is said that the female is the weaker on a physical plane, but stronger on the spiritual plane. It would seem that woman has failed miserably in the duties assigned to her, for it was her task to temper man's fighting instinct; to harmonize his tendency toward aggression.

The female represents the magnetic polarity; the male is electric. When twin souls meet after their long separation, there is a re-linking of that sacred bond that unites one soul with another. No lip service is needed; no subjective emotion. There is an interblending of the auras which automatically produce an unprecedented state of beautiful ecstasy. The love of twin-souls is a love no Earthly power can break, for it has been etched in the chambers of the heart forever.

The poets have decreed that love is the most potent force in the universe. It is the perfect, talismanic jewel. Woman was created to minister to the principle of love. Love reveals the close relationship between spirit and matter; between Earth and he heavens above.

Polarity is essential to the creation of all things. When new creation is necessary, the polarities are intensified. When heart can speak to heart in true love, then with a kiss of the soul, each half is reunited.

Many strange things have happened since the beginning of the UFO era and now it would seem that this new vibration has entered the field of romance and marriage. Perhaps it will at first be shocking to some; too utterly fantastic to be believed by others. From all parts of the globe, reports are appearing that seem to indicate that twin souls are meeting on a vast scale. Many believe their love has come from out of the vastness of uncharted space.

While visiting in an eastern city recently, I was invited to talk to a group of women (all strangers-to me). All had been through this same rapturous experience. They had listened to the voice of the "loved one," their own twin soul from somewhere out of the voiceless spheres. They had experienced love's ecstasy from beyond the limitations of Earth

Closer acquaintance seemed to indicate they were all well balanced, since-re and forthright women, their ages ranging from early thirties into, perhaps, the fifties, They showed no indication of neurosis or frustration. All admitted this new, strange love had come about unbidden and naturally. Suddenly, out of nowhere, they had been fired with the flame of love; a merger of the physical and spiritual atoms.

To listen to these stories told with frank sincerity was like hearing tales taken from the books of the Brothers Grimm. The narratives varied somewhat, but in essence they were the same. Their true love had come out of nowhere. He had come suddenly. In a few cases the experience had resulted in a break in their marriage; in other the calm regularity of their lives had been disrupted. Others told how, when the new adjustment had been made, they have found a new bond of unity in marriage.

While there is no way to properly evaluate such experiences now that the shocking effect has worn away and the evidence has had time to sink deep into my consciousness, it would appear at this point to mean the shifting of the whole physical drama. It could mean a radical change in the marital status of the Earth.

With a broadened understanding will come the proof. In the long range picture we have seen the possibility of changes in the physiology of man. We have come to realize that the time will come when human bodies will go through a definite change. They will be less dense, more rarified. If there is to be an intensification of life on all planes, the place to begin would be in the love life of the individual. New creation means new bodies. New bodies must be created through elevated status. We will not find the higher way on our present status quo, nor will we find it in decay and decomposition.

Since love is the most refining element in the universe, we need only to ignite the spark of true love to set the refining furnace into operation. We all live each day in the hope that tomorrow will make us something greater than we are. If we are unable to embrace the greater within our own sphere of living, we try to make this possible for the offspring we bring forth. As consciousness begins its ascension, it embraces the broader horizons and the more beautiful concepts. Density is diffused and an aurora of light comes in. This is eventually evidenced in the cellular body. The human form takes on a greater degree of perfection. Sensitivity is increased. Gradually, finer particles of matter replace the heavier substances.

Those who have had these amazing, stirring experiences all have the same answer: "I seemed to have merged with all life, everywhere," they say.

Mrs. I. M. of a northern California city told me her story:

"Silently and alone I walked," she said, in her low, sweet-toned voice. "The shackles of past and present were no more. The tears, doubts and fears of yesteryears were swallowed up in a peace that passed all understanding. I found myself in a corridor bathed in warm light. The glow seemed to come from everywhere; from the soft brownstone that made up the walls and ceilings of the passageway and from underneath my feet.

"Time stopped and I sensed the still, living present. Steadily, I walked into the unknown, knowing not, questioning not, where it might lead me. At last a new and unfaltering trust sustained my moving feet. Though the passage seemed unbroken, there now appeared a room or recess to my left into which my feet were guided. There, quietly awaiting me were two lovely maidens, identical in appearance. Their almost transparent olive skin and dark black hair seemed to melt into soft flowing robes of creamy white. As if in answer to my unuttered question, they spoke as one: "We are to prepare you to meet Him." Magically, all Earthly clothing dropped away and I stood unclothed and unafraid.

"In the center of the room stood a wrought-iron standard, supporting a beautiful, hand-hewn slab of wood. Now came the softly spoken order: "You are to lie upon this table as we bathe you in the precious oils." Hands light as down administered, yet seemed to touch not, as portion after portion of the cool, sweet balm was spread from head to feet. From surface to the innermost depths of my being it penetrated until every living cell had received the cooling benediction.

"With boundless joy I arose; no further promptings were needed. My soul restored to its virgin purity, I felt the stirring call. Again I entered the passageway, but no longer moved toward an unknown destiny. At last I was to meet my lover! Winged feet carried me . . . carried me on and on . . .

"Then I stood before him. I beheld him in his manly splendor. I gazed with rapturous delight upon his sweet countenance alight with the glow of the eternal. Silken tresses of blond hair fell upon his shoulders, and he was clad in beauteous raiment. Dark, luminous eyes looked into mine and spoke with eloquence and I moved into his extended arms. Time and form alike faded into nothingness as love met love, and only bliss remained. Virgin soul had united with its mate . . . Eternal living Flame . . . the Holy Spirit of All Life."

What is this pure, exulted love that seems to link two beings together by means of a sacred cord? "Fear not; for thou shalt not be ashamed; neither be thou confounded ; for thou shalt not be put to shame; for thou shalt forget the shame of youth, and shall not remember the reproach of thy widowhood any more."

When there is a uniting of twin souls, all fear vanishes and there is a feeling that nothing is impossible in the whole wide world. The story related above came from the lips of one of most pure heaven sent women it has been my privilege to meet in this life. She spills her magic of love over everything she touches. Her life has been dedicated to others. She has a wonderful Earthly mate endowed with a wealth of spiritual understanding. There is perfect harmony in their home.

Is this the mystical marriage to which sages and poets so frequently refer? Matter comes into manifestation as the result of the reaction of spiritual action. Matter is energy in the state of rest. It is the force in a state of equilibrium. In short, matter is solidified spirit.

The closer we come to the threshold of change, the deeper we must plunge to find the rational answers. Perhaps in the strange days ahead it will be a commonplace happening for beings from higher realms (or the more advanced planets) to meet their loved ones here on Earth.

We are finding some verification of this in the press. Recently word came out of England that medical men were baffled at a number of cases purported to be events in "immaculate conception." Most of the cases were discarded as frauds but, as case histories began to mount, research was begun in earnest. While the majority were disposed of as illegitimate claims, in at least two of these cases no rational explanation could be put forward. There was no evidence whatsoever of a physical father.

Perhaps we might find a hypothetical theory in the researching of the late Luther Burbank! He made the discovery that all germ plasma must from time to time have some modification. Complete change requires radical division. Luther Burbank held firmly to the theory that all germ cells (whether plant or human) must carry the same great potential. It is all part of the preparation for the big breakthrough that is soon to come. Eventually all will come forth in complete awareness.

! quote from a recent letter received from Mrs. P. J., another Californian:

"This particular part of my experience," she says, "that is, the uniting with another, began in 1951 and has been continuous since then. I know now that the soul is ever united. But to know it consciously, it must be experienced. It must be experienced through love. To the degree that I have become united with my beloved, I have also become united with myself. . . and with the whole.

"In the beginning of this experience, I was able to lay aside my intellect and my emotional self, and find that center deep within. In that state all things seemed perfect, though formless. Expression must come through the heart center ,then on up through the intellect; but in order to express there must be someone to express through. Someone who can call forth complete awareness. It is through the heart center one expresses with feeling. Response likewise is through feeling. When two twin souls are again reunited, the vibrations are stepped up. There is an ecstasy that goes beyond any words ."

One asks, is this part of our spiraling evolution? Will it in the future become an integral part of this mysterious drama of life? A part of the pattern and plan we know so little about?

While pondering deeply on these questions, I received a telepathic communication from Diane. She came in my moment of need, to clarify my doubts.

"My daughter of Earth," she said, "no, it is not an illusion of mind. Nor is it the yearning in the human heart for love. There exists a bond between beings on Earth and those from higher realms. Through the channel of love comes unity and peace. Through the channel of love comes the elevation of the race itself.

"Love is an attractive force; a beautiful inspiration," she continued. "Strange as it might seem to Earthlings, the plasmas of the higher can be transplanted in the lower. When the channels between the planes have been opened, plasmas from the higher can be transmitted through the Earthly husband. In this way, children are born of Earth, but they are not truly Earthlings. The Earth husband merely provides conditions for the offspring of true love to be born. The true parent might be an extraterrestrial, but he need not be present in a physical body."

I was grateful to Diane but I was not altogether satisfied. As further verification, an old volume, hoary with age, was mysteriously placed in my hands. Here was further proof, though abstract, that perhaps there are many extraterrestrials who have come in through so-called natural birth.

Twin souls are the absolute expression of the masculine and feminine rays. The masculine contains the feminine and vice versa. Sex is the perfect expression of the positive and negative forces. Here is balance at center.

I was reminded of two cases that had come to my attention. The offspring of the strange union, in both instances, were unusual children. The one would go into ecstatic glee when shown a picture (drawn through space) of the purported other-worldly sire. These children will be interesting case histories to watch through the years. To find one's true mate is to fit into the pattern of love like the harp to its strings. In the many personal interviews I had, the women had all seemingly touched "something." A miracle had happened. These women from all walks of life had been awakened by love to a new state of awareness. A stirring soul-quality had been born in them that had added something to the sum total of their existence. This means, does it not, that we are not entirely dependent upon material existence. It means that when the two halves of the same ego meet, whether in physical or spiritual form, a love follows that no earthly power can break. It means that the actual germ plasma from the absent one can be transmitted.

While it will take time to reconcile this type of thinking, perhaps it is the first step toward acceptance of a new reality. If it is difficult to accept the idea that beings from the more advanced planets might be sending us their love, we have only to refer to our own Holy Book:

In Genesis we find: "And it came to pass when men began to multiply on the face of the Earth and daughters were born unto them, that the Sons of God saw the daughters of men and they were fair; and they took them wives all which they chose. . .

"There were giants in the Earth in those days; and also after that, when the Sons of God came in unto the daughters of men, and they bare children to them, and the same became mighty men which were of old; men of renown."

This would seem to indicate that when the polarities are mutual, matter can become impregnated with the higher. It would seem to indicate that it is unnecessary for physical atoms to merge to produce a physical counterpart.

All of this brought back my own experience in transdimension when my soul met its mate on the beautiful planet, Venus. As I look back upon it now, I realized that it was a different emotion than any I had before experienced. It was a genuine fellowship in the spirit. There were beautiful arias in the depths of my consciousness. I wanted to cling to that last fragment of love forever. I wanted to seal it up in a sacred vault where I alone should hold the key.

In that day in 1939 I had wanted to know more about the state called marriage, for with Earthlings this happy institution was crumbling to one grand failure; a battlefield of human emotions. Certainly on Earth we need some special brand of marriage-magic.

Are we on the eve of a new genesis? A new spiral where the Sons of God will again co-mingle with the daughters of men? Is it necessary at given intervals that new life blood must come in? The nuptial couch of Earth has been defiled. Love, the beginning and the end of romance, has been blighted. The truly compatible ray between two beings is almost unknown these days. The ability for two people to blend harmoniously is rare indeed.

Are we on the eve of rising to the new creation? Most of us on Earth have come through life with a sobbing heart. Prophecy has decreed that many changes will come. It is the grave responsibility of those endowed with channelship to turn the wheel of change.

Our Earth is enmeshed in a tangled skein. The time has come to re-shape our lives. In this hour of hope we are being force to look beyond the seen for the answers. As my own twin soul once said, quoting from "Flight To Venus":

"The problem of your humanity is a grave responsibility. The Book of the Future has been opened to you. Many great changes will come. Remember, in the darkest hours, one day there will be an integration of all peoples everywhere in the universe. Out of this will come the New Social Order of your Earth."

UP RAINBOW HILL

CHAPTER TWENTY

The illustrious Rudyard Kipling once said: "East is East and West is West; never the twain shall meet." If Mr. Kipling were alive today, he might retract that statement.

Within one short generation the caste line that has divided one branch of humanity from another is fast fading out, The capacity for experience has expanded. There is a blending of things, one with the other. Out beyond the horizons the microcosm is making friends with the macrocosm. The abstract is becoming concrete and the adage, "as above, so below," seems more plausible than ever.

Rudyard Kipling, when he made this statement, was looking at the Planet Earth through the eyes of his day. Brotherhood was confined to its own limited circles. Oceans and national boundary lines divided one group from another.

Centuries ago, China built a high wall around her territorial possessions. The millions of starving humans inside the walls knew nothing of the ways of evolution. In this way China believed she was keeping intact her territorial possessions and her age-old cultures. She was invulnerable against invasion. But she was being stifled and strangled from within.

Today China's high wall is gone. The hypothetical divisions of humanity are rapidly being torn down. The way of destruction is in China's midst. At the same time, the once alien word "brotherhood" is finding its niche. The glad hand of universal fellowship is felt now and then. Creation at the "groaning stage" is making all sorts of changes. When hands can be clasped across the oceans, then the rumblings of war will cease and the spirit of brotherhood reign.

The poets have been singing the song of "brotherly love" since time immemorial. If we are to embrace brotherhood, it must become a "living brotherhood." The day of "togetherness" is here. When we can open our hearts and our minds to the wonders of the universe, we will begin to have true brotherhood on Earth. We will know there is an unbroken union between man and the stars; between human beings and all life, everywhere.

"For as the new heaven and the new Earth, which I shall make, shall remain before me," sayeth the Lord." How are we going to bring about this universal brotherhood?

The substance of the universe flows through all life. Every living thing is tinctured with the substances from below; the essences from above. In the long chainwork of evolution mankind has come up the hard way. He has stumbled and he has fallen. He has picked himself up again and gone his woeful way. Always, buried deep within him, has been the assurance that there was something brighter across the horizon. He believed there were many mysteries still undiscovered. He might have to swim in muddy waters for a time, but eventually they would clear and he would feel the exhilaration of the uninterrupted universe.

Why has man never found what he has been searching for? Because through his long sojourn on Earth he has warred for his bounty. He has been at war with himself. At some point on the globe there has scarcely been a day without deadly conflict. Man has swung with his pendulum. He has embraced the related opposites, going from war to peace, from poverty to prosperity, then all the way back again.

He has never tried to find a way to rise in peace and tranquility through that open way known as the third channel. He has preferred to tear down the walls and blast his way through. The center was there, but it was obscured in ignorance.

Human vision is widening and consciousness is growing each day. Consciousness is the substance upon which we will one day rise. But consciousness must be mixed and blended. The peoples of the Earth who went their separate ways back in the dim dawn of the present cycle must be reunited again. Perhaps it was necessary for them to be separated that they might learn the art of specialization. But the time has come to universalize.

We know that much of the true eastern culture has withered and decayed. Western territorial aggression has been slowed down for there are few virgin areas to be explored and conquered. When the essence of the cultures of the East can meet with the genius of the West, then the spirit of brotherhood, long submerged, can become a reality.

Many oarsmen are pulling up the turbulent stream today; men and women dedicated to world peace, covering every inch of global terrain. Outstanding among these trailblazers, and perhaps one of today's strongest links between the East and the west is Dalip Singh Saund, of Westmoreland, California. Two years ago, Judge Saund, Indian born and a full-blooded Hindu,
was elected to sit in the United States House of Representatives.

The story of Dalip Singh Saund fits the pattern of the American greatness that has followed a straight path throughout our history. Less than a decade ago, Judge Saund, a symbol of brotherhood between two different worlds, was an alien in our land. He was not entitled to vote. To be exact, he was an obscure lettuce farmer in the sandy, sun swept Imperial Valley of California. But in the short time that he has been a public figure, he has tried to bring the spirit of "togetherness" to our Western world.

Judge Saund was elected to his congressional office on the Democratic ticket but his staunchest followers were drawn from outside the pale of politics. He probably has as many supporters among Republicans as he has in the Democratic camp. Just prior to the 1958 elections, automobiles that carried the Republican banner two years before headlined the words: "SAUND FOR RE-ELECTION." Why? Perhaps because the heritage of the centuries is in his blood. Judge Saund does not merely stand for a principle. He is a principle.

Not one word of "smear" was used by him in his first campaign. His opponent was the beautiful and beloved Jackie Cochran Odlum, also an ethical campaigner. It was a neck-and-neck race, to be sure, for Mrs. Odlum, wife of multi-millionaire Floyd Odlum, was a "darling of the gods." Not only was she a woman of spirit, integrity, and that rare quality, intrepidity, she had come up the hard way. She was a Republican n a Republican stronghold. She was entitled to a "walkaway" victory. Yet a Hindu, unknown and unsung, usurped the vote and went to Washington as representative of California's 29th Congressional District. It was the first time a Democrat had ever been elected to this inner sanctum.

The question has often been asked: "Did Judge Saund give up his Eastern traditions to become a Westerner? No, he did not. He still is a Sikh, the one branch of Hinduism that long ago abandoned the barriers of caste. The blood that flows in his veins is the blood of brotherhood. There are many who look upon Judge Saund as a dark-skinned Abraham Lincoln. His four-sguare stand on principle has endeared him to all.

Once ensconced in the House of Representatives, he quickly became, like the late Will Rogers, another ambassador of good will—"good will between two worlds." In 1957 he made his first return trip to his native India in 37 years. He now had another problem to face; not how the Americans would accept him, but how India would accept one of its native-born who had gone over to the side of the alien. He was not at all sure of a welcoming committee, nor even a warm handshake, but he was cheered like an American hero on Broadway. He met with the Indian leaders. He told them of American ideals. It wasn't an easy task, for Russian propaganda had made the Indians apprehensive about American "equality."

Those who have followed in friendship the constantly broadening trail of this dark-skinned, tranquil mannered man from the East will tell you that he carries the mark of Lincolnesque greatness. He is a living realization of the Lincoln premise that "all men are created equal." From boyhood, Saund has clung with love and affection to the pattern symbol of Lincoln, his idol. It was his quality of fairness that elected him to the office of Municipal Judge of the town of Westmoreland in 1952.

Today we need that firm, warm handclasp of friendship across the oceans of our globe. We need men and women capable of welding world-wide friendships and fellowships between all people everywhere. There are many working quietly behind the scenes to bring about a "brotherhood of unity," for only in unity and brotherhood can we find the panacea for world peace.

Dalip Singh Saund is a man invincible in his honesty. He learned long ago in his native land how to administer and live in true principle. He says he feels certain that if we will follow the premise of equality we will have nothing to fear from Russia or the world. If we can help to build this "brotherly nucleus" within our governmental bodies, the rest should be easy. When this same rationality of principle can be applied to all departments of living, the task will be completed. With proper cooperation and coordination it can be done.

The cosmic winds are blowing, mounting rapidly toward a hurricane force. Soon the "twain of the East and the 'West" is destined to meet at last. The joining together can come out of war or, like the gentle zephyrs, it can blow in the breezes of peace. If war comes, we will be in the wake of death, destruction and tortured minds and souls. True enough, it might gorge the fortunes for a few, but even they may one day be forced to breathe in their own foul radioactive dust.

Recently, another scintillating personality stepped out of the mired mass, waving his flaming torch. Ron Ormond, a young Hollywood producer-director, took the oath of dedication and promised himself and his God that he would spend his remaining years actively trying to uplift mankind and to open the doors to a permanent peace. Ron has just returned from a year's sojourn in the Far East, where he photographed the little known mysterious and hitherto well concealed secrets behind the great religions of the Orient.

"Our reward has been one of great esoteric value," said Ron after he returned. "It justifies our profound belief that the peoples of the West will one day unfold the same great inner secret powers as their Oriental brothers."

It wasn't easy to go behind the scenes to win the full confidence of these secretive people. But Ron's sincerity and captivating personality found the magic key that opened the doors. There was no traditional missionary work, no preachments about new doctrines.

"Our objective was to foster the moral cultures of mankind," he said, "and in this way promote the wisdom of oneness and the sentiment of love toward one's neighbors. Our sole purpose was an attempt to create the brotherhood of all people, everywhere."

In his soft-spoken voice, he pleaded with the Easterners to forget about war; to blend their differences of opinion; to let go of their decaying cultures so that all might speak in a common tongue. He told them how they must all live together in peace and harmony, the rule and measurement of God's divine plan.

The plan! All over the world today that plan is beginning to take form. A substratum is being laid, the foundation for the future. The sacred tenet of Abraham Lincoln that "'all men are created equal" is the beginning of world brotherhood. Ron Ormond and his partner, Ormond-McGill, went to the Far East in search of the greatest of mysteries. They were seeking something by which the west might profit. Without torchbearers such as these there would be no progress, and without progress there can be no brotherhood. They were not out to steal the mysteries for profit, as many other Hollywoodites have done. It is their dedicated purpose to try to sell mankind on the oneness of Him we call God.

Perhaps Ron was not altogether inspired by the drama of the East. Perhaps he was born to his task. As a very little boy he developed a love for the Unknown. He believed there was something wonderful beyond the veil that would one day be revealed. As he grew older he began to dabble in metaphysical and occult sciences. It was the phenomena then; it is the philosophy and the science now. His investigation and research have brought him to the feet of the Masters. He no longer speculates; he knows. He believes he has found the great secret of how the Easterners attained greater knowledge than their Western brothers. He had always wanted to know why the holy men could walk barefoot on white hot stones. How they energized their bodies and lived without food for days on end. All of these answers he found in the Orient. Furthermore, he learned that the surface has only been scratched; that there are vast universal powers that have never been tapped. This knowledge cannot be cloistered forever. With a reign of chaos in the Far East it would seem that this is the time when the precious vaults of knowledge will be opened.

Ron Ormond was admitted to the inner sanctum of the East because the word "dedication" was written on his heart. They knew he would complete the task he had set out to do, and they were ready and willing to help him.

Ron knew it, too. He was of the West, where speed has taken precedence over all else. The West has specialized the object. Materialism has reigned. The East has specialized in the subject. Idea creation has reigned. Today the two extremes must meet at center. There must be a merger of the objective and subjective. Ron knew that bridging the gap is the first step in unity; the first all around nucleating factor in brotherhood.

Those of the West will not find their soul freedom sitting cross-legged in a darkened cave. They will not find it in the orange robes of the begging bowl. But Ron has a plan whereby the centuries-old traditions of the East can be merged with the speed of the West. The Masters have spent a lifetime in meditation and contemplation, but with science on the ascendency, Ron is certain there is a way to accomplish the same objective in weeks or months. It means finding a way to open our own individual force field to bring all bodies into play at once.

The first step is adopting the "spirit of brotherhood." As each one finds this "unity of spirit" it will begin to encircle the globe like an elastic girdle.

Young Ormond stole hours from his precious sleep to think it over. He and his partner had met the sages and gurus face to face. The two had been inspired by the holy flame from their broad and active auras. They had felt the power of Peace as it flowed through every atom of the Wise Ones. Ron Ormond knew that the unseen forces that protected them would one day protect him also.

It was a strenuous and hazardous journey they mapped for themselves.

In their sojourn they invaded the privacy of the aborigines of many countries. They met and photographed the Igorote headhunters of the Philippines. On Taiwan it was the Yamis, or nature worshippers more often referred to as the Devil Worshippers.

In Indo-China he came across an interesting group known as the Mois of Viet-Nam, a primitive aboriginal village where the inhabitants still worship the totem pole.

"These people," Ron says, "seem to have literally stepped out of the stone age into the twentieth century. They were quite absorbing and I now count them among my close friends."

However, the two partners did find their accommodations hard to take. They slept on the same straw mats and even ate the same unpalatable food as the Mois, "While they were primitive in one sense," he says, "they were certainly more spiritually advanced than we are."

In Tay-Ninh in southern Viet-Nam he found an amazing bit of modernism wrapped up in primitive cultures. It was a religion called Caodaism. Only 34 years old, it claims more than three million adherents. Furthermore, it has enthroned the Giao-Tong (or Pope), holder of the religious laws and masters of the mystic branch. There is a schematically established hierarchy of dignitaries: the Cardinals, who are chiefs of the legislative body; 33 archbishops; 72 bishops; 3,000 priests,and an unlimited number of student priests.

Ron says, "From every indication, this group of religionists gives promise of becoming one of the giants of the Orient. It is a religion based on tolerance and the worship of the true God, though He is called by many names."

Caodaism had its beginning in the crude development of channelship. Slowly, the founders crept up the ladder of the spirit until some of their followers eventually tapped in on the (fluid) true cosmic essence so often referred to by the beautiful Diane. It was then the Superior Ones became their guides and instructors. Then came the day when the summit was reached and direct communication was theirs. They met the Supreme One whom they called Cao Dai, and He brought the truth to the people of Viet-Nam.

In the 34 years of their existence, many have been initiated by the Great Master himself. The holy city of Caodaism covers many acres near the town of Tay-Ninh. This region, once dense forest and shrub, now houses a population of 100,000 persons. Dotted around the city one finds hospitals, markets, schools, printing plants; but in the center of all stands the Temple Divine. This artistically designed House of God carries an assemblage of symbols, each representing some great religion of the world. An invisible chorus sends forth its angelic strains from the tower of Sakar.

Caodaism has flourished because it is free. It holds no "fenced in" creeds or dogmas, The flag of universalism waves from its temples, and as Ron Ormond says:

"'We spent three wonderful days in the holy city, guests of the Administrative Body. It truly made me realize that our Oriental brothers are far more advanced in matters of esoteric sciences than we are. I knew too that before we can advance we must learn something of their arts and their sciences."

It would seem if this spirit of oneness is to prevail over the Earth, a primary step is the meeting of East with West. When Ron Ormond is asked why he went to the Orient when there are so many interesting places in the West to explore, he says this:

"I went to the Orient to help perpetuate the fellowship of man and bring about the brotherhood of all people. Through direct touch with the Orient and Orientals, I hope to be able to translate the great teachings of the ancient sages into English and other languages, thus giving all first-hand entry into the teachings of the wise gurus of the East. I have dedicated myself to this task, for I believe that divine knowledge is the only answer to today's grave problems. It is the one way we can unite all mankind into a Universal Brotherhood."

While his many cans of film from the East are being processed, Ron and his charming wife June are now engaged in the production of the first "true" flying saucer film entitled: "Crusade to New Horizons." In Ron's absence, June has carried on, delivering her messages from platforms, raising the necessary funds for the production, creating a life-sized script and in general being a brave little miss dedicated to bringing to the world another chapter in brotherhood.

We are no longer traveling in the ox-cart, nor are we limited to fast speeding airplanes. The call is no longer an echo in the jungle. The past century has given us the telephone, the telegraph, radio and television. They all have been channels of communications through space. Is it madness to assume that communications from the far-removed planets can be carried on with beings of Earth? Is it further madness to entertain the thought that they might be more advanced than we are, hence have a potential and ability to do things we cannot do? Of what value would it be to glimpse the far horizons if we could not find the ways and means to reach those horizons?

Let us be honest with ourselves. Have we not spurned the East because we have felt ourselves superior to easterners? Have we not looked upon them as backward, immature people? They hugged their strange, and to us heathen religions just as we hugged our transient possessions. They travelled the path at a leisurely, crawling gait, while we tried out new speeds every day.

It is not necessary that we sit in meditation on some high mountain year after year. We do not have to go into periods of silence speculating on worlds beyond our dreams. Nor do we have to martyr ourselves to some remote cause. But a little of the tranquility and quietude of the easterner might help us find that basic principle upon which they have stood through the centuries.

It is not easy to break from traditions. Through the centuries the East has held to a subjective way of life, while we have become more and more objective. Without the subjective, the objective becomes the end of the trail. These two interchangeable concepts must work toward the same creative design. Each must work toward center each in its own way.

Nature's invisible laboratory is never idle. The subtle forces have been at work for a long time. When these two forces meet, each from opposite angles, one is polarized with something of the other. The merger of the East and the West can become one of the greatest elements in polarization ever known to this Earth. It can produce a completely new line of thought that could in time become the new road of action.

It is fortunate that we have Judge Saund and a Ron Ormond to appear now and then upon our horizon. We need these ambassadors of good will. They are usually drawn from the very heart of humanity. These devoted pioneers are always simple souls, ruled more by the heart than the head. Many times they are quite unaware that they are doing a universal work.

When we have brotherhood on Earth, we will have time to open our hearts and minds to the wonders of the universe. Personality is still in command, and personality must pave the way. The progress of the human race is dependent upon both extremes, but they must eventually find a balance and hold forth at center. There always must be room for the unusual and the unexpected. Opportunity is not static. It is forever presenting itself in a new garb.

Life in the East has been going through a long siege of convolutions. Life in the West has been spiraling along the evolutionary path. The one has drawn its substance from inner sources; the other has found the keys to the golden door of materiality. Each has planted its seeds in its own way. The day of flowering came and was followed by the day of ripening fruit. But all fruit must return to its original seed.

We dare not condemn that which we do not understand. Life is for the purpose of forming and reforming. To refuse to grow is to ossify. Each serves its purpose for the term of its duration, but the time comes when its usefulness is over. The spiritual values within must be made manifest without.

When the links of the chain can be banded together in fellowship and love; when each link is related to every other link; then as the mountain-climber clings to his rope, mankind will progress on the rope of growth. These links must be made strong. There must be a tie between inner and outer. They must be individually forged. Then they must be welded together. In this way strength, confidence and knowledge are gained. This is the momentum needed to get things done.

The Earth's worn out measuring rod has served its purpose. It must now go into mothballs as a reference for oncoming generations. Man is not the barbarian he was a few centuries ago. He at least is trying to sprout wings of aspiration.

When the genius of the West can meet the refined cultures of the East; when the spirit of our "greats" can meet on the same plane with the Spirit of Buddha and the High Priests of the East; then the spirit of brotherhood, long overdue, can be born from the womb of heaven.

CHAPTER TWENTY-ONE

This is the day of miracles, but if we are to perform miracles we must believe in wonders that reach to the far horizons. The door leading to the miraculous is beyond the province of earth. It is hard to find this door unless we have some idea where we are going. The trail-blazers have been sages of wisdom, the lonely few who have travelled the way of spiritual illumination. In one expanded flash of consciousness they have seen the splendor beyond the sunset. They have taken in the whole panorama of the universe. In this briefness of a moment they have touched the realm of the all-knowing, for this is the transmuting force that pushes aside the road blocks and leads to the farthest point upwards. Here the magic founts of true, unadulterated essence are found, ready and waiting to be molded and brought forth in new form.

But the road to illumination is like the "many roads to Rome." There are many paths of diversity, but in the end they all lead to the same place. This is probably what we will find when we go out into the untrespassed sanctity of space. We will find the colors of the spectrum attuned to the musical scale. We will find radiant, living beauty, not in fantasy, but in fact. We will be able to bathe in the midst of the long-sought "golden density."

Much of the enlightenment coming through the veil has come through before, perhaps many times before. It has come in flashes of cognition, but we were not yet ready to adapt it to our use. It was theory then; it can become fact now.

With the coming of many glimpses of the Space Age, we have at last become level conscious. We are willing to give consideration to the fact that perhaps there are many space levels we know nothing about; levels we have not begun to pierce even in our mathematical calculations. Only as we begin to reach these levels can we switch on the lights.

We do know that fact is crystalized fantasy. The earth plane has been slowed down to a crystal state. Matter is spirit in earthly manifestations. We also know that our bodies are composed of flesh, bone and tissue. From the day of birth to the day of death we are seeking release from the fleshly form. Yogis and holy men spend their lives in solitude that they might experience to the fullest a release from the physical body.

Most of us accept the premise that we live in a three dimensional world, overshadowed by the fourth dimension. If other planetary vibratory frequencies are higher than ours, it stands to reason the physical shell would be far less dense, hence easier to translate into the etheric body. The "electronic body," free to traverse the lower frequency bodies would not be obliged to penetrate the rigid shell. Consequently, that which we look upon as miracles would be commonplace. Extraterrestrials would be able to transit our orbit. They would seemingly be visible one moment, invisible the next. The molecular or etheric body knows no limitations. It can translate from one form to another in a flash. The motivation of the etheric body is directed from higher, not lower fact.

The cellular or earthly body comes into being at the time of conception, the lifeline running to the point of death. While alive the molecular or etheric body is in the process of development for the next arc. This delicate and usually invisible twin is composed of tiny molecules of a frequency beyond the range of human vision. A few scattered individuals born with X-ray eyes can see the molecular body as clearly as they see the physical form.

But one need not go through the stage called death to have full cognizance in the etheric body. Released from the enslavement of earth, the body grows less dependent upon the things of earth. As the refining process progresses, the substances that compose the body become more rarefied, until a great yearning for the glorified life finally begins. As consciousness is intensified the new horizon grows broader to let in the splendor. There is a greater awareness of life and its noble purpose. It is not altogether a tranquil state. For a time, at least, one must swing back and forth between the two planes of existence. Full satisfaction cannot come until the level of human consciousness has been raised. The urge to explore other regions, other lands begins. There is an occasional release from the dense body and one can travel unhampered in the twin. A twin body carrying virtually all of the physical appearance of an earth body but created from a finer grade of material than the substances of earth. This is what Dr. Jung calls the quasibody.

Matter has undergone a state of transmutation. The new body, while almost identical in appearance, is far more pleasing to the eye because it now emanates a brilliant radiance. The energies have been refined. At this point one is aware of a third, or electronic body. This is often referred to as the "body immortal," for when one can touch the electronic body he has gained conscious immortality.

The electronic body is made up of fine, golden threads that reach out to the Great Beyond. This is the realm of miracles.

The techniques given in "Over The Threshold" served as a means of helping the reader to open the gate to the levels beyond. It aided him in becoming aura conscious. The aura belongs to the etheric body and is withdrawn from the cellular body at the moment of death. The aura serves the electronic body from above, the cellular body from below .We are the sum total of our aura. The aura knows no barriers. It can penetrate the densest of material substances. It can reach out and beyond. In the techniques given in the book it was shown that true, live color helps dissolve the irritants so that there is a free flow of energy through the various bodies.

The first step was the cleansing of the aura so that it might be rid of its pollution and psychic waste. It proved a simple method of dumping the residue back into the cosmic incinerator to be consumed in living flame.

There are psychic bacteria just as there are physical bacteria. Psychic bacteria cause congestion and hamper the free flow between the bodies.

None can deny that the Earth is tainted with foul vibrations. The task ahead is to clear away these hateful vibrations. The reading of ancient literature reveals to us that many centuries ago the aura had a more prominent place in the lives of men than it has today. At that time it was a method of communication. Some contactees believe that space beings make contact through the human aura. Like the rainbow, it is the link between the planes.

The third step in the "Over The Threshold" techniques was a means of rejuvenation; giving oneself a clean, fresh start. The next step was regeneration; transmuting the elements into "clean, pure, vital substances." Regeneration is transmutation. It means changing impure substances back to a state of purity. It is believed in this space age that color and music will lead us into the far dimensions.

Color in this sense must not be confused with the dye products known to our earth. Where is live color to be found? Live color abounds in nature and eventually it will be tapped just as the earth is tapped for its natural resources. Those who have developed extrasensory vision can clearly see these radiantly magnificent colors, for they literally flood the atmosphere with their brilliance. The ability to perceive true color comes with heightened sensitivity. Color helps to translate the beauties of other worlds. It opens the door of magic to the transcendental realizations.

The transfer of the polarities, first from the cellular body on up to the etheric body, and hence to the electronic body, requires these step-by-step techniques. First we must have a working knowledge not only of the physical body but the subtle bodies. Until we have a concrete idea where we are going and why, mere ritual will avail nothing. No amount of loquacity about "subconscious worlds" brings that realm into being. None of us have yet seen the "subconscious." Super senses have in a measure been developed to the point of actually viewing the aura not only of a human being, but of the earth. Those who have given their lives to the search are convinced that within the aura is the second body, the twin; within that a third body served by the field of electronics. They know that each body can spring into action when given the proper password.

We will not reach any conclusions while we measure on a purely earthly yard-stick. They will not be found in the laboratory test-tube. Nor will they be discovered by vacillating from negative to positive. The subject must be viewed with intelligence that goes beyond Earth science. The more rarified the material, the deeper it can penetrate. The more attenuated it is, the broader its scope, the more fertile the Elysian fields.

Density varies, just as matter varies. Earthman cannot reach beyond his solar system. He has his extremity "up." He has his terminal "down." At the uppermost point, substance is immaculately pure. There has been no adulteration. There has been no psychic pollution, nor has it touched the so-called evils. These substances are referred to in "Over The Threshold" as the "clean fresh plasmas." They are the first substances to stream from the holy founts.

We cannot reiterate too often that pure, clean plasmas begins the trek downward, going from level to level. Each step downward is like going into a fog; density is increased and poisoned radiations begin to adhere to the whirling substance. It is an accretion of pollution gathered in from the residuals and released into the vacuum of space. It is the exudations of hates, fears, jealousies and greed together with the chemical refuse created on the earth sphere. The stepping-down procedure continues until the lowest point is reached, where it becomes the vilest of matter. When this point is spanned the last atom of purity has been exhausted.

Destruction is a powerful magnet blowing its gusty smoke from the fiery furnace. It is said that one mite of clean plasma has greater potency than all the forces of destruction put together.

Substance is drawn into form by means of vibration. In our concrete world substance is drawn in from the womb of another. In the etheric realm creation is instantaneous. The invisible becomes visible with the speed of light.

A clean, color-tinted aura is a bulwark against the invasion of these unwanted, unclean substances. As set out in "Over The Threshold", one need not depend wholly upon the aura that his life's experiences have created. One can build an aura with the same etheric building blocks. It can be built to one's specifications.

UP RAINBOW HILL

The Bible states that Jesus was an Essene. Diane has interpreted this to mean he was "controller of the divine essence." Jesus had the artistry and the skill to manipulate these "pure essences." He healed the sick. He commanded Lazarus to arise from his couch of death. He fed the multitudes with five loaves and two little fishes. Jesus knew how to tap the "first plasmas." He drew this pure substance from its source by means of the golden threads streaming out from His electronic body. He had power over all matter.

Will science one day bend its efforts toward these apparent miracles?

Disease and destruction rides in today on invisible waves. It will continue to flood our earth streams until we learn how to cooperate with the universal plan. We carry not only our own created evils, but our inherited evils as well. We inhale these dense concentrates until they become a congestion in the body. This stale debris stored in the aura is the end result of disease. It frustrates ambition. It helps to keep us from reaching our life's goals. To nurse an aura filled and running over with psychic larvae is to eventually call in the doctor or perhaps the undertaker. Like a virus, it enters the bloodstream and in time is absorbed into the structure itself.

Where are we going to find an absorbent? We've tried chemicals. We've tried poisons. We've tried just about everything our planet has to offer. Color belongs to the etheric plane. It belongs to the next higher rung of the ladder. Perhaps we must look to the next dimension for the answer.

Matter is transformed by the consciousness that is put into it. With sufficient force anything can be released to its next higher dimension. On each higher level are new gradations of color. To bathe in pure color is not fantasy, but fact. We speak of matter as solidified spirit, spirit in which the frequencies have been slowed to a virtual stop. Matter arranges and transforms itself into a myriad of molds. It is from these molds that the images of Earth come forth. Diversity in form has been man's greatest ambition since his first days on earth. In the Stone, Age, he busied himself to provide shelter from the elements and in foraging for food; the simplest things of creation. Today it is difficult for earthman to realize that the things he has made for himself had their beginning in that same rarified essence he is trying to conjure from space. It is still harder for him to concede that this world of crystallized forms was once part of the world invisible. When it has run the gamut of Earth's inert slavery, it will begin its trek back to Source.

That which happens to man happens also to his world. One day the earth will be crumbled to dust, the atoms streaming upward toward the home from whence they came.

The Ark of the Covenant is a promise that the rebirth of our Earth will take place in the grandeur of rainbow colors. One day we will find our way back to the universal ethers for a bath In living beauty. Man, "made in the image and likeness of God," will be purified and sent out again on another round of cosmic experience.

All are attributes and manifestations of the One. Not one single molecule of the muck of the subworld reigns will stay that way forever. As one part of the cosmos rises, all must rise . At the change of cycles, all must change.

The techniques in "Over The Threshold" presented a simple, kindergarten method for cleaning up our house to ready it for new occupancy. The sick and unclean aura of grays, blacks and muddy browns was replaced with vivid, prismatic blues, pinks and orchid-magentas. Color ablutions are applied to the aura so that it might be washed clean to allow the pure essences to flow in. With the cleansing of the dark areas, the bright, golden light can shine. It is not only a vanguard against environmental evils that beset us each day, but a safeguard against the Earth's mephitic aura as well.

The first set of techniques covered: Elimination; Purification; Rejuvenation; Regeneration (Transmutation). When the inhibitions and blocks are dissolved there follows a release into the new freedom. Often the congealed masses crystallized in the aura represent the accumulation of a lifetime. Prayer has been the only known way to keep the aura clean. But color belongs to the etheric plane. It is the most powerful cleanser.

It is difficult for one enmeshed in materiality to visualize something beyond the physical; something perhaps more important than the physical has ever been. We are Earthlings. Our bodies are composed of Earth substances. When we go into space perhaps we will find the same set of laws. But they will have a different application.

The first set of techniques was given to absorb or blot out the debris, and the final step is the application of "pure gold." It offered a way to build an aura as bright as the noonday Sun. Golden threads run through all manifest forms. They begin at the head and reach to the farthest point in space.

As was indicated in the "Over The Threshold" techniques, a sanctuary of privacy is an aid to quicker results in the use of this new work. Comfortably ensconced in one's own cloister, the first step in getting a clear picture of the modus operandi is to visualize the three-fold body; cellular, etheric, electronic. When extrasensory perception has been awakened it is possible to see clearly the interaction between the bodies and the golden threads as they penetrate each part and parcel of the whole. Perhaps it might be illustrated in this way; a house is dark until we switch on the lights. Human beings must wander in the darkness until they learn how to switch on the electronic lights. To be able to command all bodies is to command life itself.

It is said of Nikola Tesla that his body was a virtual electrical generator. It is obvious now that he had turned on his individual electronic lights. He could command the field of electricity at will. He built his plans in the sky. He operated the motors by tuning in on God power. It is said by all who knew him that he never fitted in with Earth life.

The first step, then, is to visualize a beautiful ray of golden light, beginning from the center of the top of the head. See it fanning out in all directions until the entire visual aura becomes a blaze of brilliant radiancy. Let this golden light permeate every atom until it becomes a living, golden mist. When the "golden aura" becomes a reality one can do just about anything; command life or command heaven. It will be an experience of unbelievable grandeur.

Success may not crown our first efforts, but when the aura becomes bright with the rays of emanating light, all dross is burned away. Rather than the impure mixtures we have looked upon, we will see all space filled with golden light. We will know that in our folds of the ethers we have everything we need to remake our world. We will find the plasmas, the essences of all nature's hoard. Eventually we should be able to bring wonders into manifest form by means of direct creation.

Otis Carr has said again and again that we cannot go into space until our individual force field has been built. This is one way the individual force field can be developed. It will have the power to dissipate gravity and clear the avenues of space.

Today we are attempting to step out into the untrespassed zones of the upper ethers. We are looking to the virgin fields for our "manna from heaven." This will be the greatest stride in human advancement. People the world over are being caught up in this flaming spiral. The links are growing stronger. We must look for help from on high. Without help we can do nothing.

CHAPTER TWENTY-TWO

Earthman stands as a pivot surrounded by Life. His measurement and his growth has nothing to do with the books he has studied, nor the university scrolls that decorate his walls. He can be proud of his accomplishments, to be sure, but this is all part of the garment of civilization. The true measurement of his knowledge is how he fits into his environment; his rapport with all life, visible and invisible. It is the subtleties that count. If his aura is magnetic he can attract and bring forth from higher realms. Perhaps he might make a living touch by way of channelship with another planet.

The communications system followed on Earth is carried out also in higher planes of existence. Channeling means one's ability to come into concord with those unseen; to be compatible with invisible forces; to become mediators. Channelship is tuning in. We "tune in" in much the same way we flip the dial on a radio. But rather than tuning in by way of mechanical means, one makes the connection through human sensitivity. The capacity for potential, for reception, while often natural with particular individuals can be developed by all. When one has not had such an experience and so is unable to embrace it mentally, it is difficult to entertain such an idea. That same individual who is skeptical of channeling would have rejected the idea of radio or television without substantial proof.

The non-sensitive knows nothing of the remote regions of space and his mind is unable to perceive such places. To such a one, the realm of other worlds simply does not exist. But when the time comes for the tangible reality to appear, the skeptic embraces it without questioning. Once he can see it, taste it, or feel it, he takes it for granted, and curiously enough he does not think about it as coming from the beyond or in any way that it is linked up with the Universal All.

Channeling is a word that has come into broad use because of space contacteeism. Before knowledge can be dispatched through space, it must be channeled. Channeling is bringing to a focus so that a result might be obtained.

In contacteeism the vibrations of the cellular body are lowered, the vibrations of the etheric body heightened. Following natural law, it is normal to assume extraterrestrials have mastered the secret of channeling long ago. There have been many great epochs in the history of man. In each one of them he has had to learn to climb on the golden threads. It is not hard to accept the premise that each planet differs in its rate of vibration, its color, and its potentiality. With much new knowledge being released, countless channels have been made all along the way. It is no longer the individual, but the groups who are important. In every group there are "potential" channels. There are hidden talents. Group consciousness helps to bring them out so that they can become manifest.

Space is the subject of the great experiment today. What with rockets, sputniks, missiles, and much talk of exploring the moon, we are forced to recognize that there may be more ways than one to prove our theories. Perhaps basic principles will have to be reserved. Earthman has been taught to work from facts upward. Scientists pride themselves on their untiring efforts to coax the innermost secrets from facts. The men in this group think nothing of spending years examining a grain of sand in the hope that this minute particle will bring forth some great revelation.

What are facts? Fact is a mere crystallization of a point in space. When we go beyond facts we go to the source of all facts. Working from facts out into the unknown requires the ability to stick to a single point. It means diligence to a task. Working from totalities or absolutes is a reversal of that principle. The result is obtained by raising the consciousness to a point of rapport with the source. It means the "togetherness" rather than the apartness. Einstein found the principle in relativity.

In working with facts, our scientists penetrated the depths of matter coming up with the split atom. Nikola Tesla worked from totalities downward. He tapped the source of electronic energy. Edison, on the other hand, worked from fact. The one was an inventor, the other a creator. Otis Carr hopes to lead us through density into that glorious golden world we have not yet glimpsed.

Facts are the offspring of principle. Without principle (without the invisible) there would be no manifest fact. We have given our wholehearted attention to facts, forgetting the realm where the facts originate. Again, we are trying to measure other planets on the old yardstick. We are not taking into consideration that each planet may have its own individual keynote.

We are living in the midst of grave danger. Is it not worth our time to give thought to the alien if this might be our way out? We would like to return to the "good old days" but those days have passed forever. We cannot go back.

The thought of radical change is always upsetting. Otis Carr has attempted to answer this question, at least in so far as free energy is concerned. He says:

"The introduction, manufacture and use of OTC free energy will bring more prosperity to more people in the United States and throughout the world than any single invention in the entire history of the world."

Power is the fuel of civilization. How our world is powered is how our world will be. Diane once told me that in the interim of change and complete breakthrough there will come a time when money will be abolished as a medium of exchange; money will no longer have value. In that interim we shall be forced to draw our sustenance from the higher founts. Jesus fed the multitudes on essence-created elements. Moses fed the pilgrims on "manna from Heaven." Perhaps the coming of free energy is the forerunner of this great change! Perhaps it means the tapping of another universal essence. The time may come when all things and commodities on our planet will be as free as the air we breathe.

Free energy is not an element that is yet to be discovered. It is everywhere present. When we learn how to channel free energy it will serve all our needs. In the many experimental laboratories across the globe, the primary factor needed to harness this mystery, is focus. Some are feeling their way with the quartz crystal. Others are experimenting with the prism. In the human realm the third eye is the focal point of contact. It is located in the center of the forehead just above the bridge of the nose. The third eye is often referred to scientifically as the pineal gland and, a vestigial sensory organ. In ages past man had this eye open. With the close of the cycle it must be unsealed and put to use.

Lower forms of life have been forced to adapt to different rates of vibration. The lower forms of life had to build bodies to conform with environment. Perhaps we, too, will have to build bodies capable of traveling into space. Rather than bending our energies to material comforts and Earthly greatness, when we have a free-fueled world we will devote those same energies to the needs of the Space Age.

It has taken millions of years to traverse this kingdom. We have come up through a slow-motioned ponderous Earth. When we finally find our place in space, we no doubt will cease to live in a "time world", but in rapidly speeding "space world." Adaptation will not require countless thousands of years, but will probably be made in "the twinkling of an eye."

This has been a cycle of specialization. It was right and fitting we should begin from the seedling and grow into the tree. Universal patterns would have been very confusing to those who were dedicated to the microscope and the telescope.

But the curious one asks: "Where did the seedling come from? What is the origin of the tree?" During cycles of specialization evolution is stressed. In cycles of universalization, convolution is stressed. Universalists are springing up all over the world. May are suddenly aware they are no longer mere citizens of one country or another, but they are citizens in the World Universal. This is the first stages of brotherhood, the beginning of the universal language. The spirit of brotherhood felt deep within is part of the New Age pattern. It is one of the lessons we must learn before we begin our climb UP RAINBOW HILL.

We cannot put "new wine in old casks." Neither can we use the materials of one cycle to serve another. The old pieces will not fit into the new pattern. Man's physical body was built to provide him with the things of Earth. His physical organism was created out of the materials found on this planet. He is part of his place of birth.

We are being prepared today to meet a strange, new world. But before we can plunge ahead there must be some point of contact. Something or someone must make that contact. There must be preparation. Every new kingdom must be prepared for in advance. For this reason every means possible is being employed by space beings to reach the masses. There are hoaxers, to be sure. The hoaxers creep into any new field. But they eventually discredit themselves. It seems now that the final proof will be the degree of channelship an individual is able to evidence.

Nor is there at this time any way to bring forth proof such as the world can understand. All we can do is theorize rationally, and out of this rationality will come truth. It it can be assimilated by the mind, it has the potential to become a reality. That the UFO movement has mushroomed to gargantuan proportions should be evidence enough that it is something we dare not ignore. If we do, the task will have to be done over at some later date.

Inspiration is at high pitch. It is no accident that hundreds of New Age books are appearing and that the message is being shouted from many rostrums. Once we can be drawn up in consciousness to that realm where peace abides, then we will find the transforming, transmuting power we have been seeking. Perhaps we will actually tap that one substance out of which we can remake our world. The vital energies of nature will be waiting to serve us. We may be able to build new bodies; a new life. At the center of all things we will find the kernel. This is the point of center. When the shell is pared away we will know the meaning of transmutation. When the white heat of desire is generated, the rest will be easy, for desire is stronger than necessity.

Is this one of the answers to the great enigma? If, as Doctor Jung seemingly has suggested, they are-quasi-human beings, does this mean they would not be able to adapt to our planet? That they will never walk the streets of our cities? Not at all. But it would doubtless mean our frequencies will have to be raised and theirs lowered. Just as the lung-fish became a land creature, a quasi-body could eventually become in all ways earthly. If it is true that they have gained power over the one substance, the adaptation to our frequency would be an almost instantaneous process. At any rate, it certainly would not require centuries as with less evolved life. By means of the speeded-up vibrations, the changeover would be complete in a relatively short space of time.

When matter is translated into molecules, the density is released and it leaves a fine, wraith-like substance. When the molecular body is played upon by electrical fire it is quickly reduced to invisibility.

Evolution proceeds by building up and tearing down. Under the persuasion of the higher vibrations convolution would be brought about by means of electronic energies. Just as Earth life has come up through a long evolutional chainwork, the lower forms of life being forced to adapt to varying rates of vibrations. Once we plant our feet on the higher rungs we will learn to build bodies capable of traveling in space. When there is union of two planes, we can look forward to enlarging our spheres of action.

The ethers contain everything we need to build the new life. Perhaps we will find more wonders there than we could ever hope to find on this ponderous earth. The same cohesive substance binds all. As substance goes through the furnace of fire it is refined and, as its vibrations slow, it crystalizes. It is all one and the same substance. It all had its beginning in the higher founts of purity. The man who declared: "I will only believe that which my eyes can perceive," is too ignorant to know that beyond his sensibilities lies the true reality, the invisible pattern. Without the invisible, without the molecular and electronic, there would be no visible, or cellular form.

Mystics tell us that deep in the bowels of matter we find the offensive stables of depraved souls. Sensitives who have dared to venture into these lower hells speak of unbelievable horrors. One asks: "How can an entity survive in these subworlds, deprived of cleansing elements like pure air and water?"

A human being could not survive, of course. These soul saddened creatures must live in these grottoes of darkness until their time of change comes. When the cycle is ended, these evil entities will be given another chance. Some believe these dark grottoes have existence somewhere in the lower regions of the earth. The only light ever seen here is the flame from Satanic fires. In this state the consciousness becomes fossilized, it is swallowed up in inertia. Only a terrific pressure from above can dissolve these concentrates. It is the same substance that once started from its source, pure and uncontaminated, but in its trek through time has become thoroughly foul. These residual evils give off an emanation of violence.

War and destruction has made a deep groove. It has fogged our vision and dulled our finer faculties. Consciousness is group strength; one helping the other. In group strength there is power. Many today are doing a wonderful job in trying to loosen up the debris so that more light might stream in. In this way, the roadways into space can be opened.

A vast orbit remains to be explored. The area must be surveyed with an inner yardstick before we attempt to transport ourselves into space. We would not attempt to push one of our clumsy battleships into the etherian waves. Perhaps it would be just as unavailing to encase a human body in a few hundred pounds of lead. We know we cannot take our gold mines and our oil wells into space. If we are going to go on the quest for bigger bounty, we'll also have to leave behind our lavish estates, our race horses, and our minks. We would soon find out that none of these values would fit into the greater scheme.

If we continue to measure other planetary realms on our short yardstick it might be many more centuries before the breakthrough can be accomplished. If we can think it, it can be done. That we can even conceive it means that mental channels have been opened up. When we review our accomplishments, they stand out like an array of soldiers on parade. The achievements of the future seem remote to us now, but when we think of them as possibilities, one by one these possibilities will become manifest.

When we forge our way beyond our gaseous, treacherous atmosphere, we will be amazed by our new discoveries. We will doubtless find that it will not require years to travel the millions of miles between one planet and another, but that the trip will be made in virtually a flash of time as we know it. The change will be as radical as that of the Stone Age compared to present day civilization. Earthlings will see themselves as new beings who have come out of a dense and slow-motioned planet. Perhaps they will sing divine anthems from the depths of their hearts.

Mystics have told us that Earthlings will one day inherit the bounties of Venus. They have told us that our bodies will appear much as they do now, but drafted on a more perfected pattern. All things must follow the same advanced plan. Nothing remains wholly static. The higher arcs of creation mean the attainment of a higher stage of advancement. Diane has said we can have wisdom, truth, and knowledge beyond anything we have ever known. But first we must cleanse away the debris that holds us to the lower Earth. Many are busy today trying to find a more progressive way to mold the original plasmas into form. Those who reach toward that "just-beyondness" will eventually find what they are searching for.

If there are planets more advanced than Earth, they have progressed because they have become more aware. Those who claim contact are not extra-special people. They have nothing extraordinary to contribute to the field of knowledge. They are aware that changes are in the making. They are ready to let go of the old and embrace the new. Some of them are beginning to feel the spirit of brotherhood deep within. Eventually they will be able to speak the language of brotherhood.

The cosmos is immense and too all encompassing for any of us to understand entirely. We can move forward only a link at a time. We can drink in only a little knowledge at a time. When we can completely adopt the up building realizations; when we are willing to become whole centered and true, then we will be better fitted to attempt to measure the vastness of the universe. We will then wave the magic wand of a science born of principle, not transient fact.

This is part of the elementary education we are receiving from On High. The marching parade is on its way. It is part of evolution and growth. How we live today will determine what we can expect from the future.

We have had many past warnings. We are warned again and again.

The siren will continue to wail, growing louder and louder up to the very eve set for destruction. We all know our gravest danger lies in the enormous stockpile of nuclear bombs. Only a miracle can avert the blast. We know they cannot be peacefully destroyed without leaving destruction behind them. This is our great peril. So long as a single war minded individual remains alive on the planet, we will be in danger. Each wave of impetuous brute force brings us closer to a tidal wave of tumult that can wash us from the face of the Earth.

We must begin by blotting out violence. Wean the brute force out of man and he will ascend. He will wear the halo of the gods, signature that his individual force field has been opened.

So long as we believe in miracles, they can happen. We are all feeling the paroxysms of pain that accompany a crumbling cycle. We feel the hermetic nostalgia that covers us like a shroud. Perhaps it is an unconscious longing for that place in the sky!

In this period of rebirth those who are willing to assume responsibility must be ready to act on a moment's notice. There are those who believe that thousands of ships stand ready for the exodus. Perhaps one day we will find ourselves over the threshold basking in new world splendor. If we can transcend the cosmic scale, we, too, will be transformed.

We have achieved the pinnacle of material greatness, but its cost could be the ruination of our civilization. Expanded consciousness is the leaven that can save us. Before we can expand our consciousness we must broaden our vision. When we can elevate our minds to that point where quarreling and war can be turned back to embers, then the gap will be filled in with an ecstatic substance. We will refuse admittance to violence. In that day death will have ceased to be the dreaded monster. The body will no longer take on the appearance of age. The harrowing tortures that have been part of Earth growth will have been transcended.

The greater acts as a powerful magnet to the lesser. It increases in intensity until the time comes to be absorbed into the Great Light. Winged messengers from space brought us the message. They left it on humanity's doorstep. Sensitive channels the world over are delivering it to the various destinations. Many believe with their hearts and souls that space beings have come to prepare the way for us; to create compatible vibrations so that we will no longer be forced to grope through the fog.

There are many facets to a diamond. There are many divisions in a circle. There are many steps UP RAINBOW HILL.

THE END
OR
THE BEGINNING?

DANA HOWARD'S SPACE CONTACT WAS A BEAUTIFUL, BLONDE, EIGHT FOOT TALL WOMAN WHO MATERIALIZED IN FRONT OF A ROOMFUL OF PEOPLE

ALL ABOARD!

The great Golden Age Of Flying Saucers – complete with encounters that bordered on the outrageous – ran from the early 1950s for just about a decade. During this period, dozens of individuals came forward with seemingly farfetched stories of having established an ongoing relationship with benevolent – almost angelic – beings from outer space. With a few exceptions, these contacts took place in the desert regions of California and Arizona, and sometimes the proud earthlings that became known in pop culture as "contactees" were honored by being invited inside the exotic, airborne circular "foils" of the visitors for a test ride into outer space. Some even insisted they had stepped out onto the worlds from which their newly found ET friends had arrived.

Some of the best known names from the Golden Age of Flying Saucers include George Adamski, George Van Tassel, Truman Bethrum, George Hunt Williamson, Howard Menger, Orfeo Angelucci and a farmer named Buck Nelson who with his dog Bo established a strong bond with the space beings who landed quite regularly outback of his farm in the Ozarks.

For the most part the UFO contactees were men, but Dana Howard was a rare exception. Her first contact transpired in 1939, about which she said:

"Still wrapped in the warm intoxication of the spirit, my vision was directed to a gnarled old tree overlooking the antediluvian hills. Leaning casually against the grotesque trunk was a woman being of unsurpassed loveliness. Her head was radiant with a crown of fire, strands of golden hair cascading gently over her beautiful, slightly olive-tinted shoulders. The strange mystic light flooding her dark, prophetic eyes added a wistful something to all her other charms."

This is when Dana Howard noticed a strange object suspended in mid-air about three hundred feet above the ground. "In the main it seemed to be constructed of some sort of translucent materials, but trimmed in gold, and gem-studded. An almost invisible ladder extended from the ship to the earth, and I obediently followed the radiant being up the filmy stairs without questioning."

It wasn't until sixteen years later that Dana had her second encounter when the same radiant being materialized in front of a group of individuals gathered for an occult workshop in Los Angeles. By this time New Age philosophies were being widely accepted and so no one cringed or got "spooked out" when this beautiful being appeared out of thin air and announced that she was from Venus and wished to speak directly with Ms. Howard. What followed was an ongoing series of contacts that lasted for several years and culminated in a series of UFO contact books by Dana Howard, including the classic you are now holding in your hands which has been unobtainable for more than fifty years.

Order Up Rainbow Hill
for just $21.95 + $5 S/H

GEORGE HUNT WILLIAMSON'S
THE SAUCERS SPEAK'
OTHER VOICES

In 1951 George Hunt Williamson was doing anthropological field work among the Chippewa when he began to hear the many legends of the "Hairy-Faced Men," 'Gee-By's" (ghosts), along with countless tales of the 'Gin Gwin" or that which shakes the Earth. These "Earth Rumblers" might also be known as "Flying Wheels" or "Flying Boats."

The author of Other Tongues Other Flesh began to realize that such "tales" were common place among many other native tribes. This fascination with 'Flying Saucers" lead to actual radio contact with Extraterrestrials that was repeated time and time again in front of credible witnesses. His privately published report on these ongoing communications attempts to "speak" with beings from other worlds has – over the years – been duplicated by others and has been the subject of highly classified debate in scientific circles.

OTHER VOICES (ie Saucers Speak) includes Wiliamson's full findings as well as a complete update which includes no less a famous individual than the late Senator Barry Godwater who often stated that both the U.S. and Russia had "picked up such (unknown) signals before..." and that 'NASA is doing research into this." In recent times, ordinary citizens have heard messages over their households radios and have even received strange pictures on their television sets that have NOT been aired by any normal broadcast facilities.

Order OTHER VOICES for just $15.00 + $5 S/H

OTHER TONGUES OTHER FLESH REVISITED
BY BROTHER PHILIP
(PEN NAME OF GEORGE HUNT WILLIAMSON)

Order OTHER TONGUES - OTHER FLESH REVISITED
for just $24.95 + $5 S/H

INNER LIGHT, BOX 753, NEW BRUNSWICK, NJ 08903

Write checks or money orders to Timothy Green Beckley

Write checks or money orders to Timothy Green Beckley

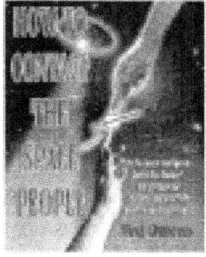

Write checks or money orders to Timothy Green Beckley

UP RAINBOW HILL